ISBN 978-1-332-84260-5
PIBN 10184725

This book is a reproduction of an important historical work. Forgotten Books uses state-of-the-art technology to digitally reconstruct the work, preserving the original format whilst repairing imperfections present in the aged copy. In rare cases, an imperfection in the original, such as a blemish or missing page, may be replicated in our edition. We do, however, repair the vast majority of imperfections successfully; any imperfections that remain are intentionally left to preserve the state of such historical works.

1 MONTH OF
FREE
READING

at
www.ForgottenBooks.com

By purchasing this book you are eligible for one month membership to ForgottenBooks.com, giving you unlimited access to our entire collection of over 700,000 titles via our web site and mobile apps.

To claim your free month visit:
www.forgottenbooks.com/free184725

English
Français
Deutsche
Italiano
Español
Português

www.forgottenbooks.com

Mythology Photography **Fiction**
Fishing Christianity **Art** Cooking
Essays Buddhism Freemasonry
Medicine **Biology** Music **Ancient
Egypt** Evolution Carpentry Physics
Dance Geology **Mathematics** Fitness
Shakespeare **Folklore** Yoga Marketing
Confidence Immortality Biographies
Poetry **Psychology** Witchcraft
Electronics Chemistry History **Law**
Accounting **Philosophy** Anthropology
Alchemy Drama Quantum Mechanics
Atheism Sexual Health **Ancient History**
Entrepreneurship Languages Sport
Paleontology Needlework Islam
Metaphysics Investment Archaeology
Parenting Statistics Criminology
Motivational

LIFE AND CHARACTER

OF THE

HON. JOHN C. CALHOUN,

WITH ILLUSTRATIONS:

CONTAINING

NOTICES OF HIS FATHER AND UNCLES, AND THEIR BRAVE CONDUCT

DURING OUR STRUGGLE FOR INDEPENDENCE,

IN THE

AMERICAN REVOLUTIONARY WAR.

~~~~~

NEW-YORK:

J. WINCHESTER, NEW WORLD PRESS,

30 ANN-STREET.

SUN OFFICE, CORNER FULTON AND NASSAU: J. C. WADLEIGH, 459 BROAD-
WAY: BRAINARD & CO. BOSTON: ZIEBER & CO. PHILADELPHIA: WILLIAM
TAYLOR, BALTIMORE: GEO. JONES, ALBANY: J. B. STEEL, NEW
ORLEANS: AND BY BOOKSELLERS & PERIODICAL AGENTS
THROUGHOUT THE UNITED STATES.

PRICE 6¼ CENTS.

LIFE AND CHARACTER

OF THE

HON. JOHN C. CALHOUN,

WITH ILLUSTRATIONS:

CONTAINING

NOTICES OF HIS FATHER AND UNCLES, AND THEIR BRAVE CONDUCT

DURING OUR STRUGGLE FOR INDEPENDENCE,

IN THE

AMERICAN REVOLUTIONARY WAR.

NEW-YORK:

J. WINCHESTER, NEW WORLD PRESS,

30 ANN-STREET.

1843.

PREFACE.

WE believe, with many of Mr. CALHOUN's friends, that neither his public or private life is as fully known among the mass of our fellow citizens as it deserves to be.

We have in the following pages, in much haste, thrown together many of the most prominent traits and circumstances which have marked the career of himself and ancestors; and we have endeavored to point out those actions in his life which go to prove him one of the most distinguished of men, the ablest statesman, and the most extraordinary man of the age in which we live—whose reputation will descend to posterity as that of a great and good man, when the prejudices and false impressions, cast around him by over zealous opposition, shall have passed away for ever.

It is a circumstance worthy of note, that, among all the present candidates for the Presidency, Mr. Calhoun is the only one whose family were involved or took any active part in the Revolutionary War; while he himself contributed largely to bring about and to sustain the late contest with Great Britain. It may also be noticed, as an interesting fact, that his father served thirty years, and the subject of this sketch thirty-one years, in public life—making a period of sixty-one years for father and son. To maintain the uninterrupted confidence of their constituents for such a length of time, argues a high degree of merit and integrity on the part of both father and son.

THE AUTHOR.

NEW-YORK, November, 1843.

HON. JOHN C. CALHOUN.

~~~~~~~~~~

THE father of John C. Calhoun was Patrick Calhoun, from Donegal, in Ireland, who emigrated to America before the Revolutionary War. The family of Patrick first settled in Pennsylvania, and afterward removed to Virginia, where he married a lady by the name of Caldwell, the mother of John C. Calhoun, and whose family, also, came from Ireland. After Braddock's defeat, Patrick Calhoun, being driven by the Indians from the western part of Virginia, in 1756 removed to Abbeville District, in South Carolina, where John C. Calhoun was born on the 18th of March, 1782 ; he being the youngest of five children—four sons and one daughter. He was named after his uncle, Major John Caldwell, whose assassination by the Tories in the Revolutionary War, we shall have occasion to speak of, in another part of this work.

To understand the hardships to which Mr. Calhoun's family were exposed, prior to, and during the Revolutionary War, it is necessary for the reader to bear in mind the position of the country at that early period of our history.

In 1756, we find there were thirteen weak and scattered colonies, with a population of little more than two millions of people, without good roads, or means of ready communication—with the rolling ocean on one side, and a dark wilderness on the other—filled with powerful tribes of Indians, inflamed against them by the emissaries of France ; while the mother country only regarded them as fit subjects for future taxation and oppression. Under these gloomy and adverse circumstances, our first settlers had little else to depend upon, beyond the help of God, and their own stout arms and brave hearts. From Maine to Georgia, for years, the borders of the colonies, now called the old thirteen States, presented an unbroken and bleeding frontier, where men were compelled to work their fields in sight of *log block-houses*, with their rifles by their sides, ready to rally at the first alarm, in defence of their wives and children. It often happened, however, that the Indians suddenly surprised and cut off whole families and communities, leaving utter desolation and ruin in their train. The history of those troublesome times is full, of villages sacked and burnt—of women and children barbarously butchered and scalped, and whole settlements depopulated, by the most savage, wild, and ferocious foe, with whom man has ever been called to contend against; and whose known mode of warfare was distinguished by cunning and cruelty, and so conducted as to deceive and to destroy their victims, sparing neither age or sex in their fell swoop of destruction. We read of Indian wars and bloodshed in the Far West, at the present day; but the tribes that now remain, are weak and softened by incipient civilization—their worst acts of cruelty being far behind those inflicted by the more powerful and barbarous tribes with whom our forefathers, in their hour of trial and weakness, had to withstand. Even the Cherokees—now a small, and one of the most civilized tribes—in the early settlement of the country, were found to be the most cruel in the torture of their victims; while the stake and the faggot were the instruments of death used by all. To fall into their merciless hands, was to be burnt alive at the stake; and, by this horrible mode of torture, hundreds of men, women, and children, suffered the most painful deaths. Those were times, indeed, "that tried men's souls;" and they were just such times as *old Patrick Calhoun* had the soul and the courage to meet and stand up against. With a heart as brave as a lion, he was always found at the point of danger, and ready to do battle for his country. He had fought the Indians on the western borders of Virginia, till the period of Braddock's defeat, when the combined forces of the Indians and French poured upon the defenceless settlements in desolating fury, and compelled the scattered inhabitants to fly for safety before their approach. Among other families forced to yield to a foe flushed with victory, and eager for the extermination of all whites in their way, was that of old Patrick Calhoun, who sought a home in Abbeville, South Carolina. But here he found he had pitched his tent in the face of an enemy still more powerful and ferocious than any with whom he had yet contended. The Cherokee Indians were now his near neighbors, and could bring into the field a powerful array of warriors. They inhabited all the country west and north of him, and were ready, at any moment, to make a descent upon all the whites within the State. But, in this beautiful part of the world old Patrick Calhoun had fixed his home, and he determined, by the help of God, to defend it, if it should cost him his life. And defend it he did, both against Indians and British; and, when full of years and full of honors, was buried on the farm his industry had improved, and his valor had secured.

He had not been long at his wilderness residence in Carolina, before he and his neighbors were called upon to rally in defence of their homes. The Cherokees, excited by evil influences, were led to meditate an attack on them; and having approached the settlements in large force, ready to do their work of destruction, the alarm was given, and all the male persons able to bear arms were rallied, and old Patrick Calhoun placed at their head. When his gallant little body of men were brought together, their whole force amounted to only thirteen! But every man was *true grit*, and a stranger to fear. Their old commander had a soul as warm as fire, and as large as a barn, and which was as brave as it was warm. He, without waiting for the Indians, at once led his men forward to meet them, and, if possible, to fall upon them by surprise. After leaving their w   s and children to the care of God and their country, they went forth to an uneq   nd bloody contest—and a majority of the little force were doomed never to ret n again in this life. When old Patrick, with his small band, had penetrated in the dark and silent depths of the forest, seeking stealthily for the wary foe, he suddenly met them, and became immediately engaged in deadly combat. Old Patrick was foremost in the fight, urging on his followers to the struggle. *Seven* of his men—more than one-half of his brave little troop—lay dead around him. Himself, and six others, were all that remained. The Indians appeared in overwhelming numbers. Old Patrick made a careful retreat, and saved his remaining men; while the Indians had met with such a severe resistance, that they thought it prudent also to leave the field, and retire from the settlements. When old Patrick returned to the battle. ground with his men, to bury their dead companions, they found the lifeless bodies of twenty-three Indian warriors.

BATTLE OF OLD PATRICK CALHOUN WITH THE CHEROKEE INDIANS.

Many other exploits and conflicts between the whites and Cherokees, might be detailed, in which old Patrick Calhoun took an active part, had we time to relate them. His superior skill and bravery in Indian warfare, like that of General Jackson, had become as famous among the Indians as among the whites. They knew and dreaded his power. In those days, no settler ever ventured out on a hunting excursion, or for any other purpose, without his rifle, accompanied by a good supply of powder and balls, and a large knife at his side.

Old Patrick, on one occasion, took down his gun for a stroll in the forest alone, and during his rambling, suddenly met a Cherokee Chief. Each knew his man. The Indian, as soon as he saw old Patrick, sprung to a tree, and screened himself behind it, while old Patrick threw himself down behind a log. They were both dead shots; and whoever fired first, should he miss his aim, and afterward be visible to the other party before he could reload, he would receive the deadly ball of his antagonist. The position of each was extremely critical. To all appearance one of them had to die: their chances were equal; and nothing but successful stratagem, contrived by great presence of mind, could give either party an advantage. The least imprudence, or failure of marksmanship, would have resulted in a loss of life. In such an emergency, none but a cool and brave-minded man, accustomed to meet savages in battle, could expect to come out victorious. In this trying situation, we find old Patrick Calhoun equal to the dangerous circumstances in which chance had suddenly placed him. In order to draw the fire of the Indian first, he placed his hat on the end of a stick, and gently raised its crown above the log, behind which he lay; on perceiving which, the Indian mistook it for the head of old Patrick, and fired his rifle at it, but still retained his position behind the tree, not certain of the success of his fire. Old Patrick again raised his hat when the Indian had reloaded, and again drew his fire. Still the chief feared to expose his person. This was continued till the fourth fire was drawn, when, the chief supposing his balls had slain his antagonist, stepped from his concealment so as to expose himself. The moment was auspicious for old Patrick, who levelled his rifle with an unerring aim, and lodged his ball in the shoulder of the chief, who, finding himself seriously wounded, took to precipitate flight. On examining his hat, he found it pierced with four bullet holes.

OLD PATRICK CALHOUN FIGHTING A CHEROKEE CHIEF.

During the whole of the Revolutionary War, we find old Patrick was a substantial and active patriot. South Carolina, in proportion to her population, suffered more seriously in our struggle for independence, than any state in the Union. Before the rupture with Great Britain, she had peculiar advantages of trade allowed her, and it was a favorite colony with the mother country; and had less to complain of than any other of the thirteen.

The rich products of Carolina were eagerly sought by British merchants, and Charleston early became one of the most important and flourishing seaports in America. But, when the Carolinians heard of the scenes passing in Boston, and of the battles of Lexington and Bunker Hill, their feelings of sympathy and love of liberty were aroused. And there was no colony among them that went into the contest more clearly on PRINCIPLE than South Carolina. While the people of the northern colonies were proscribed by British power, and the port of Boston was closed, no act of the mother country was ever specially levelled against the people, or the pecuniary interest of this State. The people of this colony, therefore, went into the war with everything to lose, in the way of property, and nothing to gain but *liberty*. It was PRINCIPLE for which they contended. When told they had no reason to complain, that their taxes were nothing compared to the advantages granted by England, their patriotic cry was, "We have millions for defence, but not one cent for tribute."

So lenient had the home government been to the Carolinas, that, at the breaking out of the contest, a number of the more timid colonists took sides with her, and became the most cruel and bitter foes the patriots had to meet during the war. They were at all times, and in all places, considered even worse than the English.

When the British army took possession of Charleston, they immediately adopted the most severe and rigorous measures toward the patriots of this colony, consider. ing them the most ungrateful of all the subjects of *King George the Third*. It is not our purpose to go into the history of those troublesome times. They stand re- corded in the most sacred archives of our history.

In the same proportion as the British inflicted cruelty, confiscation and death, on the unfortunate colonist who took up arms in defence of their country, in the same ratio were the patriots inflamed with resolution and courage. A lady in Charleston, when she found the British were about to take possession of the city, set fire to her own house. When it was besieged, the ladies worked with their own hands on the trenches and breastworks. They also attended the sick and wounded of the army; supplied them with clothing and food, and both nursed and dressed their wounds. When the city fell into the hands of the English army, they shunned the so. ciety of British officers, and sought out their countrymen in the dungeons and prisons of the town, and administered all they could to their comfort. It was a dark day for Carolina; some of her best blood was made to flow like water for the cause of free. dom. It was about this period that the brave and gallant Col. Hayne was led out to execution, by order of the bloody-minded Lord Rawdon, and whose premature death cast a gloom over the whole nation. From Charleston, the English spread over the Carolinas, and made a complete conquest of the country. Lord Raw- don, wherever he went, carried death and desolation before him; all the unfor. tunate Whigs who fell into his hands, whether by Tory craft or British warfare, were, in most cases, ignominiously hung or immersed in dungeons, and chained to their floors; or were made to endure sufferings more terrible, in some instances, than death itself. Amid these bloody scenes and wide-spread conquests, there were a few men who kept the field in spite of all attempts made to defeat and capture them. The brave Sumpter and Marion, with handfuls of men, living in swamps and pine forests, subsisting on potatoes and other scanty fare, still held out for their country, and were always on the alert, and ready to strike a blow when an oppor. tunity presented itself. Among the brave men who held out faithful to the end, and never failed in his duty, was *old Patrick Calhoun*. He had to defend his home against Indians—and now for seven long years we find he was ranged on the side of the patriots, fighting for the liberties of the country?

At the close of the war, we find old Patrick occupying high ground among his fellow-citizens, who reposed the greatest confidence in his honor and courage.

Before saying more respecting this brave old man, we will turn to the members of Mr. Calhoun's family on his mother's side—the *Caldwells;* all of whom bravely joined the patriot cause, and rallied to the support of their country's standard. The eldest was *Major John Caldwell*—the uncle after whom, as we have said, John C. Calhoun was named.

This uncle became early a conspicuous officer in the ranks of the soldiers of the Revolutionary War, and excited the deadly hate of the Tories. In those days the Tories were both the murderers and plunderers of their own countrymen, struggling for liberty. They generally asssociated in small bands, under leaders of the most cruel and abandoned character, who paraded through the country, pillaging the houses and destroying the property of all the Whigs that fell in their way. They were, generally, a cowardly set, and always avoided a contest with the Whigs, unless the odds were greatly in their favor. They were despised even by the higher class of English; officers and were only used as tools and spies, to do the vilest and lowest acts of villainy. They were mostly Americans, and a disgrace to the country which gave them birth. Whenever the Whigs were absent from home, they sought an opportunity to approach their dwellings and rob them of everything valuable they could carry off; and completed their work of destruction by mur-

DEATH OF MAJOR JOHN CALDWELL.—See next page.

dering women and children, and sitting fire to their houses. They, often, on finding a Whig at home, on leave of absence, either shot him on the spot, or carried him off to the British, for imprisonment or execution. We could go on, if our limits

permitted, and relate many horrid deeds of cruelty committed by these marauding
traitors, during our war of Independence.

Major Caldwell was a Virginia gentleman of high respectability, and had adopted
the cause of his bleeding country with that ardor and devotion peculiar to the tem-
perament of the race of people from whom he had sprung. He was in the prime of
life, and had a high and responsible part before him to act, in the perilous affairs of his
country. His course was decided. Liberty's banner was unfurled, and he rushed
to the rescue. When accidentally at home, in the bosom of his family, surrounded
with all those comforts of life secured by honest industry, and encircled by all the
tenderest ties and relations of domestic life, the approach of armed men was heard.
He rushed into the yard to see who they were, when a band of infernal Tories
fell upon their unarmed victim and, assassinated him in front of his own door. Not
content with this deed of murder, they set fire to his dwelling and reduced all to
ashes, while his helpless family were forced to fly to the fields and woods for protection. Thus perished one of *John C. Calhoun's* uncles, in the prime of life and
manhood.

At a time when Lord Rawdon had proclaimed that South Carolina was recon-
quered, and had firmly planted himself in Camden, after the defeat of Gen. Gates;
and, when Lord Cornwallis was preparing to pass through North Carolina and
invade Virginia, a commander appeared in the southern field, on the patriot side,
whose bravery and skill were a match for the best officer in the English army—and
that man was old *Daniel Morgan*, the *Wagoner General*, as he was called. With
a regiment of riflemen, and an infantry force under Colonel Howard, of Maryland,
aided by the cavalry under the command of *Lieut. Col. Washington*, he made an
attempt to relieve a place called *Ninety Six*, then embracing Abbeville and Pendleton, in South Carolina, and then the residence of old *Patrick Calhoun*, and at present
the home of the subject of this memoir. Gen. Morgan had acquired great skill in fighting both Indians and English with his brave riflemen, who were present at the battle
of Saratoga, and the surrender of Gen. Burgoyne. We find him now hovering on the
advanced forces of Lord Cornwallis. In the gallant little army of General Morgan
was YOUNG CALDWELL, a brother of Major *John Caldwell*, and the second uncle of
John C. Calhoun. No sooner had Lord Cornwallis heard of Morgan's march upon
Ninety Six, than he sent a strong detachment of his army to attack him, composed
of 350 men under Colonel Tarleton, a part of the light infantry of the 7th regiment,
the first battalion of the 71st, accompanied with two field pieces of artillery. The
British, in their infantry, had the advantage of *five to four* over the Americans.

The two forces met at a place called the *Cowpens*, near a small river, in South
Carolina, called the *Pacolet*. At first the British seemed to gain the advantage, but
brave old Morgan's riflemen poured in such a deadly fire on the foe, aided by Col.
Washington's attack on the forces of Col. Tarleton, that the scale of victory
was soon turned in favor of the Americans. In the midst of the contest *young
Caldwell* was slain on the field of battle, and closed his earthly existence while his
brave companions were filling the air with the glorious shouts of victory. Thus
nobly perished, in a noble cause, this brave uncle of John C. Calhoun. In this
well-fought battle the British had ten commissioned officers, and one hundred rank
and file killed, two hundred wounded, twenty-nine commissioned officers, and about
five hundred privates taken prisoners. Two pieces of artillery, two standards, eight
hundred muskets, thirty-five baggage-wagons, and upward of one hundred dragoon

horses, fell into the hands of the Americans; while the latter only had twelve men killed, and eighty wounded. One of the twelve killed was young Caldwell. This

DEATH OF YOUNG CALDWELL AT THE BATTLE OF THE COWPENS.

triumph, at a most gloomy and disastrous period of the American war, proved of the greatest service to our cause. It gave fresh courage to the brave patriots, and caused them to rally in defence of their country with fresh vigor and renewed energy, that

IMPRISONMENT OF CALDWELL IN THE DUNGEON OF ST. AUGUSTINE.

never relaxed afterward till the complete and perfect independence of the country was acknowledged by Great Britain.

Mr. Calhoun's third and last uncle, Caldwell, and the remaining brother of the two deceased Caldwells, also espoused, with the same zeal and courage, the cause of his country, which marked the character of the whole family. He marched against the British; but, unfortunately, in some manner not fully known, was made a prisoner of war, and was treated with the greatest rigor and closely confined. For nine long months he was chained in a dungeon at St. Augustine, in Florida—a place badly provided with the ordinary comforts of life, and, in a hot climate, liable to engender disease in the confined air of dark and damp prison cells.

The long struggle finally terminated. We became an INDEPENDENT NATION OF FREEMEN, and were left free to make our own laws and appoint our own rulers; and, for the first time in the modern history of man, the great experiment of the capabilities of the people to govern themselves was commenced.

The first thing to be done was the formation of laws regulating suffrage in the several States, with movements for forming free constitutions under which to act. In South Carolina there was a party in favor of confining the right of suffrage to a property qualification. This proposition roused the feelings of old Patrick Calhoun, who still survived. He determined not to submit to such an aristocratic measure; and being dstermined to defend the right of suffrage at all hazards—and failing, by arguments, to convince his opponents of the justice of his cause—and seeing they were determined to open a poll contrary to what he conceived to be justice and law, he shouldered his rifle and rallied his neighbors, who also seized their arms; and,

OLD PATRICK CALHOUN MARCHING IN DEFENCE OF THE RIGHT OF SUFFRAGE.

placing old Patrick at their head, they marched to the place appointed for holding the polls, within twenty-three miles of Charleston, and compelled a change of the plan of voting. This act made old Patrick so popular, that he was, thereupon, elecetd a member of the State Legislature, in which body he served for a period of thirty years; and, like his son, enjoyed the uninterrupted confidence of his constituents as long as he would agree to serve them.

In March, 1782—in the year after the battle of the Cowpens, which was fought in January, 1781—and in the year after the battle of Guildford, fought in March, 1781—and in the year after the surrender of Lord Cornwallis, at Yorktown, on the 17th October, 1781—*John C. Calhoun*, the youngest child, and son of old Patrick, was born, as we have stated. Being the youngest of old Patrick's children, he was the favorite and pride of the old man's heart. But the noble old patriot dropped off before young Calhoun had received his education, and he was not spared to witness the future success and distinguished honors held in reserve for his favorite son, who seems to have inherited all the native vigor peculiar to the old man, marked by the same frankness and decision of character, chastened by superior education, and long and laborious study. Of the early days of young Calhoun, we have not time to dwell. As his father had left his family in rather narrow circumstances, he would not agree to leave his mother, to pursue his studies, until the elder brothers entered into some arrangement which might afford him the means of obtaining a thorough education, without trenching upon any resources necessary to the comfort and happiness of his aged mother. This being accomplished, and after having exhausted the means of instruction then at command in that part of his native state, he left for Yale College, at New-Haven, Connecticut. He set out with a full determination to make thorough work of whatever he engaged in, saying, " he would prefer the life of a farmer, to being a half-informed lawyer or doctor." At College he soon distinguished himself as an assiduous student, and made rapid progress. He set out to qualify himself for any station in life, if possible, to which his fellow citizens might see fit to call him. He is one among the very few of our American statesmen who have made a science of public affairs, and qualified himself by his education, and by a laborious and studious life, for the dignified and elevated profession of a statesman.

When he graduated at College, he received the highest honor in his class; and acquitted himself with so much success in argument with Dr. Dwight, that the venerable President predicted he would, one day or other, be President of the United States. On returning home, Mr. Calhoun entered on the study of the law; in which he soon took high rank. He afterward became a distinguished member of the South Carolina Legislature.

In 1812, while quite a young man, we find him a member of the House of Representatives of the United States Congress, and an active and leading member of the Committee on Foreign Relations. It was a most important and critical time in the history of our country. It had become evident, that, before we could enjoy our independence in peace, another conflict had to come off with Great Britain. From the close of the Revolutionary War, we had been looked upon by the proud monarchies of Europe, in the light of successful rebels. They seemed to consider that we had accidentally gained our independence by the aid of the French, and the diversion of English forces in foreign wars; and that, in case of a second and single-handed contest with Great Britain, we should be completely flogged, if not reannexed to the British crown. These opinions of our strength entertained abroad, caused us to be treated with contempt by several nations, while others made no scruple to invade our rights whenever it suited their convenience. Several powers refused to acknowledge us as an independent nation—among whom, was Austria. At one time, the brave General *La Fayette* lay immersed in the prison of Olmutz, within the dominions of Austria. Our countryman, *Huger*, with *Bolman*, were thrown into a loathsome dungeon, for attempting the rescue of *La Layette*. We then had no minister at the court of Austria, to plead our cause, or to interfere in behalf of General La Fayette and the gallant young men who attempted his release. Among the foremost to insult our flag, and to injure our property on the high seas, were the English. In short, we were kicked and cuffed about on all sides. England claimed the right to search our vessels and impress our seamen at pleasure; and, at the commencement of the late war, three thousamd of our brave tars were laboring in the British service, into which they had been forced. Our commerce had been pillaged under the Berlin and Milan decrees. Mr. Jefferson tried an embargo, which only had the effect to injure ourselves, to create discontent, and to lessen our patriotism and self-respect.

When Mr. Calhoun took his position in the American Congress, his clearsightedness at once discovered, that, if we wished to maintain our rights and independence as a nation, and compel others to respect them, we must fight in their defence. His first move, therefore, in 1812, when on the Committee of Foreign Relations, was to urge Congress to declare war at once against Great Britain, the chief offender. He considered all non-importation and embargo acts as worse than useless. He joined his committee in reporting a declaration of war against England, and advocated its expediency and necessity in a strain of patriotic eloquence that has never been surpassed. In the height of his appeal to the patriotic pride of the country, he exclaimed—" I would prefer a single victory over the enemy, by sea or land, to all the good we shall ever derive from the non-importation act. The memory of Saratoga, Princeton, and Eutaw, is immortal. It is there, you will find the country's boast and pride—the inexhaustible source of great and heroic sentiments. But what will history say of restriction? What examples worthy of imitation will it furnish to posterity? What pride, what pleasure will our children find in the events of such times? Let me not be considered romantic. This nation ought to be taught to rely on its courage, its fortitude, its skill and virtue, for protection. These are the only safeguards in the hour of danger. Man was endowed with these great qualities for his defence. There is nothing about him that indicates he is to conquer by endurance. He is not encrusted in a shell; he is not taught to rely upon his insensibility, his passive suffering for defence. No, sir; it is on the invincible mind—on a magnanimous nature, he ought to rely. Here is the superiority of our kind; it is these that render man the lord of the world. It is the destiny of his condition, that nations rise above nations, as they are endowed in a greater degree with these brilliant qualities."

After a long and hard-fought struggle, war was declared on the 18th of June, 1812, and that by a single casting vote. It was late in the season of a long and anxious Session of Congress, before the Republican party were enabled to carry this most important measure. The administration was opposed, in the adoption of this great and patriotic movement, by men who have since filled, and now seek the highest offices in the gift of the people. They were then found standing—not in the Democratic ranks—but in opposition. Mr. Calhoun performed a most important part in sustaining, and carrying through Congress, this great national question. It

DECLARATION.
OF
WAR
1812

JOHN C. CALHOUN REPORTING THE DECLARATION OF WAR.

is believed, without his aid, the bill could not have passed, as he, beyond doubt, by his labor in the Committee, and his eloquent speeches made in its favor in the House, largely contributed to its success. And his distinguished services on this occasion were lauded by the Republican papers and people, from one end of the Union to the other. Even the Richmond Enquirer was most lavish in praising the splendid and patriotic efforts of Mr. Calhoun, at that time. In proportion as he was praised by the Republicans, the more was he abused and slandered by the Federalists; and it is remarkable that none of the latter party have ever, during his public life, forgiven him, or have any one of them ever been found in his support—while large portions of them have occasionally rallied in the support of almost every other candidate for the Presidency. Mr. Calhoun never acted with them, and not a man of them has ever acted with him.

During the late war, the name of a *Democrat*, or a *Republican*, meant something; but now-a-days the title is prostituted to serve the purposes of faction, or to give a false label to *federalism*, in order to sink its character before the people. Nobody now-a-days, calls himself a *federalist*; and why? Because our glorious defence in the late war, and the complete vindication of our rights, at home and abroad, made the name excessively unpopular with the people. The federalists now call themselves *Democrats*, with *an alias or two;* but they are federalists still. They were so on the 12th day of June, 1812, and on the 8th day of January, 1815, and will be so to the end of the chapter. To call a party *Democratic Federalist*, is about as appropriate as to call the Tory party in England *Republican Tories.*

Mr. Calhoun has been a *Democratic Republican* during his whole past life, and will be so to the day of his death.

When the war commenced, it found us unprepared; and, in our first contest on land, we were worsted. But our little navy rode gallantly out to sea, in the face of the greatest naval power in the world. They soon engaged the enemy in battle after battle, and gained victory after victory. The charm of England's naval invincibility was broken. The proud title she had assumed of being mistress of the seas was disputed by us, and successfully set aside.

Our brave Jack tars, excited by feelings of sympathy for their messmates who were compelled by their captors to take up arms against their native homes, and burning with enthusiastic patriotism, they nailed their colors to the mast-heads of their ships, and sought out the English on the highways of the deep; and, under the motto of "free trade and sailors' rights," they filled the world with the glory of their deeds. The splendid naval engagements in which our vessels of war were engaged, imparted universal joy to the Republican party of the country. On every side was heard the names of Hull, of Lawrence, of Rogers, of Perry, of Porter, and other brave men. The same spirit which animated the commander and crew of the *Constitution* in their glorious action with the *Guerriere*, animated the bosom of every officer and sailor in the American Navy.

When we review those brilliant events in our country's history, we, too, are ready to exclaim, with Mr. Calhoun—"Give us one victory by sea or land over the enemy," to all the embargo acts that can ever be imposed. The memory of our naval triumphs are now as immortal as "Saratoga, Eutaw, and Princeton." It is in them we find cause for our country's "boast and pride." If there was any American bosom that did not vibrate with the general joy of the nation at the result of our heroic naval actions, at the time they transpired, it was found among the *Federalists* of that period. To them, victory was a source of regret. They, alone, opposed the war, with a zeal worthy of a better cause. They not only took sides against the war, but did all they could to put down our most patriotic members of Congress who advocated it. Their opposition rose so high, that they seemed, for a time, on the brink of going over to the enemy. These were the men who opposed John C. Calhoun then, and these are the men who oppose him still, in whatever ranks they are found. And these are the men, who rejoiced not when the loud huzzas of our victorious tars came over the sea to our shores. These are the men, who rejoiced not when the western wind bore on its wings Perry's triumph on Lake Erie. These are men, who wept not when *Lawrence* expired, saying, with his dying breath, "*Don't give up the ship!*"

Our success on the ocean infused new life into our people, and they soon began to feel their renewed importance as a nation. Owing to [the want of fortifications and other defences along our sea-coast, the English were enabled to invade us at several points, and burn some of our towns, and inflict other outrages unbecoming a civilized nation! Owing to this cause, they were successful in reaching Washington, and blowing up the capitol, which was a source of humiliation and regret to the whole country. But the act aroused the energies of the whole nation, and we began rapidly to recover lost ground on land, which continued until the great victory obtained by General Jackson at New-Orleans; soon after which the war closed, by our obtaining an honorable peace from Great Britain.

Our experience and progress as a nation, since the late war, has fully established the wisdom and expediency of that measure. In that conflict, we proved to the world that we could measure arms, both by sea and land, with the most powerful nation—and that, too, single-handed. By the honorable and brave defence of our rights in that contest, we rose at once to the front rank among the nations of the earth. Our flag now waves in every sea, and is respected throughout the world. Our brave tars are as free as the ocean-bird, and fear no opposition from a foreign soil to "free trade and sailors' rights." We now have a minister at the court of Austria, and at every other court in the world, civilized or barbarous; while old England honored us with a special minister in the person of "a noble lord." Throughout the old world and the new world, the bare name of an American citizen is a passport to respect and consideration. The writer was, in 1840, on a visit to *Liege*, a large town in Belgium. He went to pay a visit to the Government Citadel, or Arsenal. It was on a Sunday morning, and it so happened that he had no introduction, or person to introduce him. On presenting himself at the gate, and asking admittance—"From whence do you come?" was the interrogatory. "I am the countryman of Washington!" was the reply. "Enter, sir; you are at liberty to view everything within these walls. We reverence the name of Washington, and respect the country from whence you come."

We suppose all will admit the great advantages which have been acquired by this country, in the way of trade and extension of commerce. It has given us an invincible navy; it has put our whole country in a state of defence; and has tended, in many ways, to advance the country a half a century beyond what it would have been without this "second war of independence," as it is often justly called.

During the whole of the war, Mr. Calhoun never relaxed or abated in the exertion of his labor and talents in its favor; and, at its conclusion, we find him called by Mr. Monroe to fill the office of Secretary at War. On entering upon its duties, he found its affairs in confusion, and that its financial disbursements had been wastefully applied. He soon introduced order and economy in all its arrangements, and succeeded in discharging its high and responsible duties with an ability and success that has never been surpassed, if equalled.

He had seen and felt the humiliation of the country, arising from the defenceless condition of our sea-coast during the war which led to the capture of Washington, and the destruction of our Capitol, and determined to use all his influence in putting the country in such a position of defence as to prevent a future contingency of the kind.

At this period, General Bernard, who had been a great engineer under Napoleon, and who had, by his direction, erected some of the most complete and powerful fortifications in Europe—specimens of which are to this day seen with surprise and wonder at Antwerp and other places—arrived in America, an exile from France. Mr. Calhoun lost no time in availing himself of his services. General Bernard was placed at the head of our engineering corps, and went on to plan and execute a chain of splendid fortifications reaching along our sea-coast from Maine to Louisiana.

During the late difficulties growing out of the settlement of the boundary question, and the trial of McLeod, the complete state of our defences on the sea-board had the effect to make the English Government ponder before they determined on hostilities. One of the best guaranties for peace consists in always being prepared for war.

Mr. Calhoun has been accused of sectional influences and partialities. Look at the splendid forts that line the harbors and coasts of the northern States, beginning with the State of Maine; and viewing those great works of national defence, erected at a cost of millions upon millions, in the harbors of Boston, Newport, New-York, Philadelphia, and Baltimore, do they indicate sectional feelings? In this great expenditure for defence, his own State came in for a less share, in proportion to population, than any other on the sea-board. Mr. Calhoun, while Secretary at War, was never found to proscribe merit and honesty for opinion's sake: and in all his appointments he looked to superior qualifications alone, regardless of sectional birth, or of honest differences of political opinion. During his public life, as Secretary at War, or as Vice President of the United States, no one has ever charged him, in a single instance, of showing the least partiality for one section of the Union over another. Whenever filling an office in the administration of the national Government, he has always discharged his duties as an executive officer of the whole nation, and never as the officer of a class, or of a section of the country. No man ever retired from the War office with greater popularity than Mr. Calhoun. He stood among the very foremost in the Republican ranks; and nothing but his youth (being only about forty years of age) prevented his being then put in nomination for President, and elected as the successor of Mr. Monroe. In Pennsylvania, which has always been a Democratic State, Mr. Calhoun was almost the unanimous choice of the people for that high office. But Mr. Calhoun, not WISHING TO DIVIDE THE REPUBLICAN PARTY, *caused his name to be withdrawn* as a candidate, and afterward was nominated for the office of Vice President, on the ticket with General Jackson as President; and, as large as the vote stood for General Jackson, Mr. Calhoun obtained a still larger vote for the Vice Presidency, and was elected almost by the common acclamation of the whole country.

The office he now held had been occupied by worthy and talented men; but it was enjoyed rather as a sinecure, at a salary of $5,000 a year—the incumbent being content to remain at home, satisfied with the honor of the office, without feeling it necessary to attend at Washington and preside in person over the deliberations of the Senate. Previous to his election, that dignified body had generally elected one of their own members to preside over their proceedings. The Hon. Mr. Gaillard, a Senator from South Carolina, for years filled the President's chair in the Senate. No sooner had Mr. Calhoun been installed into this high official station, than he gave notice that he should preside in that body personally; alleging as a reason, that he was opposed to receiving the emoluments and honors of an office without taking upon himself its responsibilities, and the personal and faithful discharge of its duties, however onerous they might be. During the whole term of his office he was always found at his post, and presided over the deliberations of a body of men, possessing a dignity of character, a degree of wisdom and experience, not surpassed if equalled by any other assembly of men in the world—and with the most extra-ordinary success, efficiency, and impartiality; and that, too, during a period of un-paralleled excitement and difficulty. Throughout his active Vice Presidency he won the praise and admiration of friends and foes, and no one ever accused him of the least partiality, sectional or otherwise. What better proof do we want that he would make as able, and efficient a *President.* If he has been faithful, over a few things, he will be no less so as " a ruler over many." After thirty-one years of ar-duous public service, he has retired to his farm, where he is engaged in dispensing hospitality to his friends, and in enjoying those social relations of domestic life, which have always been so fondly cherished and cultivated by him during relaxations from the toils of public life.

Mr. Calhoun has never been poor or rich—he has always been independent in his resources; and while many public men have, by devotion to public affairs, let their private matters fall into embarrassment, Mr. Calhoun has always acted upon those maxims in private life that he has advocated in his official stations; that is, freedom from debt, strict accountability, and reduction of expenses within the legiti-mate sources of revenue. He was never one of those kind of men to preach one doctrine and practice another. What he professes in public life, he practices in his daily private walks. He always desires his acts, public and private, to speak for themselves; and shuns public exhibitions of himself, and public declamation for electioneering purposes—stating he considers the OFFICE of *President of the United States* of too high and dignified a character to be sought at the hands of the people by way of stump speeches and electioneering tours; and that, as it is the highest office in the gift of the people, they should be left free to make their own unbiassed choice of a Chief Magistrate.

Although Mr. Calhoun is not poor or rich, he has always been liberal in dis-pensing aid to others in distress and need. But his charities have been so privately bestowed that they never came to light, unless divulged by those who have parti-cipated in his bounty. He has always shown a deep interest in the education and advancement of young men. It is well known that the celebrated *George McDuf-fie* was born of obscure and poor parents, inhabiting a log hut in the pine woods of Georgia. When quite a lad, he strayed to Augusta, where he entered a retail store as a clerk. Here he was seen by a brother of John C. Calhoun, who had gone to Augusta with his wagon from Abbeville. On conversing with the lad, he formed so favorable an opinion of his understanding that he invited him to go home with him, and promised to use his influence in getting him placed in a more advantageous situation. On their return to Carolina, Patrick Calhoun, the brother, introduced young McDuffie to John C., who also formed so high an estimate of the young man's abilities, that he at once proposed to place him at the Academy of his brother-in-law, where he accordingly went at his expense. While here, he made the most rapid progress, and soon qualified himself to enter the South Carolina College at Columbia. Here he also prosecuted his studies with distinguished suc-cess, at Mr. Calhoun's expense. He afterward studied law, and became, as we all know, a distinguished man. On one occasion, Mr. McDuffie, with Judge Huger, the present U. S. Senator from South Carolina, were both members of the State Legislature. The subject of an appropriation to the State College at Columbia came up for discussion. It was opposed by some members from the upper counties of the State, on the ground that it had never done any good, and was only open to the sons of the rich, &c. Judge Huger rose in reply, and stated, " If the College had never educated but one man, and that man was George McDuffie, it deserved all the money the State has ever bestowed upon it."

When the judge took his seat, Mr. McDuffie rose, and said he felt deeply sensible of the compliment which had been paid him; and however much he was indebted to that institution for his education, and however much he might owe to it for the little distinction he had gained in public life, he wished the honor of his education placed where it belonged. Whatever degree of usefulness his exertions had fulfilled, or whatever honor might await him in future life, it was all due to Mr. Calhoun. It was he who had educated him at his own expense, and to him he wished all the honor awarded.

But for this disclosure of McDuffie, no one would ever have heard of the transaction from Mr. Calhoun himself. This public and grateful acknowledgement, made to a noble benefactor, was as honorable to the recipient as it was creditable to the bestower of the benefaction.

We have heard of other similar acts of kindness to other young men, which, at present, we do not feel at liberty to bring before the public—as the author of them has never, himself, let them pass out to the world, nor do we believe it is his wish they ever should do so.

We thus see, although Mr. Calhoun's means were never large, yet he has so managed his private affairs as always to maintain his family in independent circumstances, at the same time he has been most liberal in aiding the progress of others. It was said by Washington, that he considered a man, who proved himself incapable of managing his own affairs, was not a fit person to be intrusted with the business of the public. On this maxim Mr. Calhoun has always acted. And he never requires the performance of a duty, or lays down a landmark for the guidance of others that he is not willing strictly to comply with in his own personal intercourse, both in private and public conduct.

It is not supposed that our greatest and purest men can escape censure. The worst enemies Mr. Calhoun ever had, have not been able to find a flaw in his private life, or to successfully impugn his motives, or doubt his patriotism as a public man. That he has, during a long course of public life, been led into some errors, which more mature experience in the working of our institutions has corrected, he has had the frankness to admit. He is not superhuman; and to err, is the lot of man. But, as he justly remarks, his " Errors have bent to the side of his country's cause."

It is an evidence of a great mind, and one possessed by Washington, in common with other great men, to be open to conviction, to profit by experience, and carefully and wisely correct erroneous opinions, however maturely and conscientiously formed. It is a mark of weakness, of ignorance, or of obstinacy, to persevere in a course which more enlarged observations and trials have shown to be wrong. When we consider that many apparent judicious measures, recommended by wise statesmen, are found in their practical operation inexpedient, or even injurious, and that, in the movements of a new government like ours, where many important principles have, for the first time, been called into action, and are constantly effecting unexpected changes, In a country, too, that is every year marching rapidly on in

its growth, rendering useless, or injurious, some measures, and requiring the adoption of others to meet new exigencies.   Constant attention, modification, care and
watchfulness, is necessary on the part of our statesmen, as time develops the
movements of a great and free nation.   When we consider all the changes which
have transpired in our country during the thirty odd years of Mr. Calhoun's public
life, the wonder is, not that he has changed at all, but that he has changed so little, when compared to many other great men.   The advance of our republic has, in
many instances, fulfilled the early predictions of Mr. Calhoun, with a truthfulness
that almost imparts to them the spirit of prophecy.

A great noise has been made, by his enemies, about his nullification doctrines,
when it is well known, that while they are condemned by people who know nothing about them, they are yet practically acted upon by States which deny them in
theory.

When the English claimed that McLeod should be given up to them without a
trial by the laws of New-York, the General Government made a demand upon
New-York for the delivery of McLeod.   This demand New-York considered the
General Government had no constitutional right to make, and therefore *nullified the*
DEMAND by going on to try McLeod; and if she had found him guilty of murder
within her jurisdiction, she would have hung him.

When Georgia condemned an Indian, under her laws, for murder, an appeal was had
to the United States Supreme Court: a writ was sent out from that Court, to suspend
the sentence; but, before it could be served, the Indian was hung.   In the same way,
Pennsylvania, Massachusetts and Ohio asserted and maintained their State rights, in
opposition to the assumption of federal power, not granted in the Constitution.   Suppose a case: we do not say such ever will, or can happen; but, for the sake of
illustration, suppose a large majority in Congress were to determine to interfere with
the business of New-York, and claim to exercise powers within her borders, not
granted by the Constitution, and which are " reserved to the States and the people
thereof, respectively."   Suppose Congress to pass a law, ceding or selling one-half
of the State of New-York, without her consent, to the Government of Great Britain,
to be annexed to the Canadas: or pass a law to abolish the Judiciary system of the
State, and direct that all crimes now amenable to the State laws, should be tried by
the United States Courts.   Ask yourself what would be the remedy in this case?
Would the State appeal to the United States Court as a defendant, at which an unconstitutional *Congress*, or the General Government, the servant and creature of the
States, having no existence except that granted by the States under the Constitution,
should appear as plaintiff?   This would be placing the *creature* above the *creator*.
What, then, would be done?   Is there no constitutional remedy?   Must the State
succumb, or disunite herself from the Union?   Is there no middle ground in such
an extreme case?   Mr. Calhoun, in *simple theory*, thought, with Mr. Jefferson, that
in such a case, the State would be justifiable in disobeying such extra constitutional
laws; and this she might do, and still remain in the Union, under the obligations of
the Constitution.   In the case supposed, no one doubts but New-York would do as
she did in McLeod's case, i. e., nullify the unconstitutional interference of the General Government, in matters she had never delegated to that Government, under the
Constitution.   And if she appealed to any tribunal, it would be to a constitutional con-
vention of her sister States, where, if they gave a constitutional decision against
her, she would be bound to acquiesce in such final arbitration.   Yet, for professing

this plain, simple, Jeffersonian, Republican, States'-rights doctrine, Mr. Calhoun's character has been blackened with abuse, and his whole life held up in a false light before the public. Even admitting his former approbation of Mr. Jefferson's doctrine—for he, not Mr. Calhoun, was the author of nullification—would he thereby make a worse President? Would he be less able, impartial, and patriotic in that office, than he was as Secretary of War, and Vice President of the United States?

Mr. Calhoun has been charged with being ultra in his opinions, and particularly on free trade. No man is less ultra, in anything, than he. He is no enemy to manufacturers or to their interests. He is a sincere friend to American industry, and to American labor in all its various ramifications. He is in favor of all the protection which may be afforded by a liberal revenue tariff. He is a friend to working-men and mechanics, and is anxious to have all labor rewarded. He always feels the warmest admiration for, and deepest interest in the great mechanical and scientific improvements of the age; and is delighted at the proud triumphs of the human intellect over the laws of matter. He rejoices over the progress of mankind in arts, in agriculture, in commerce and in manufactures. But he, with many other wise men, conscientiously believe there is no grant in the Constitution which authorizes Congress to grant bounties or protection directly to one class of our fellow-citizens, at the expense of another; and even the advocates of the principle of protection do not claim it under any express grant of the Constitution; but whenever they draft a bill to *secure protection*, it is always headed as a bill *for raising revenue*, and they thus indirectly obtain what the Constitution nowhere, in express terms, permits.

During the whole course of Mr. Calhoun's public life, he has been known conscientiously to contend for a strict interpretation of the Constitution; and has always opposed every attempt to gain, by indirect means, objects which that sacred instrument does not directly grant. This, we take it, is the true republican doctrine. If a door is once widely opened to this kind of indirect legislation, in favor of measures unauthorized by the plain letter of the Constitution, where is the evil to end? What is the use of the Constitution at all? The future glory and prosperity of this nation, depends upon maintaining inviolate the provisions of that holy chart of our liberties.

However urgent and strong the expediency of a law may appear, the whole nation may even groan for it; yet it is far better to suffer, to groan for a time under the heaviest burdens, than to inflict the most fearful and greatest of evils by deliberately stabbing or violating the Constitution of the country. If evils arise that must be redressed, or measures are proposed which promise great and extensive benefits to the people at large, and are calculated to "promote the greatest happiness of the greatest number," and no grant is found in the Constitution by which such evils can be redressed, or such measures adopted, let the people, if they choose, amend the Constitution, or, if necessary, change the Constitution by the action of State Legislatures, so as to meet the cases which it is proposed to act upon. But, come what may, through evil and good report, whatever else is done or proposed, let us maintain inviolate the Constitution, that sacred inheritance, transmitted to us by our forefathers.

We have thus briefly brought under review the history of a man and his family, who, by their brave actions in defence of our country and its liberties, have identified their names with the first patriots of the land—a family whose elder branches fought and bled in the first conflict for freedom—and of a younger member of that family, whose best days have been employed in the service of the Republic, and who aided in bringing about, and in carrying the country triumphantly through the second war of Independence. We feel our inability to do justice to this great man. To write out a history of his life, would be to give a history of the country for thirty or forty years of its progress.

In conclusion, fellow-citizens, we recommend John C. Calhoun to you, conscious that, if he were personally as well known over the whole country as he is to his immediate acquaintances, he would be as much beloved by the whole nation as he is by them. We recommend him to you as a long-tried and faithful public servant —as an honest man—as a true patriot and upright citizen—and as a man every way qualified for the *Presidency of the United States*. Then let us give three cheers for the memory of *old Patrick Calhoun*—three cheers for the *three Caldwells*—and nine cheers for *John Caldwell Calhoun*.

THE END,

CPSIA information can be obtained
at www.ICGtesting.com
Printed in the USA
LVHW011358111218
600055LV00004B/438/P

WALLY LEARNS A LESSON FROM TINY TURTLE

Written by Carolyn Webster-Stratton, PhD.

Wally was really excited because the baseball season had finally arrived. He was crazy about baseball. In fact, he had an awesome collection of baseball cards and he knew the names and batting averages of most of the players. Often he fell asleep at night with his baseball hat on.

2

Sometimes he bragged to his friends at school about being a famous baseball player one day.

"I'm the best player, I can swing so fast. I can hit a ball so far out of the field that I get home runs most of the time. I bet you can't do that."

Freddy replies, "So what's the big deal? I think soccer is much more fun - you don't have to stand around and wait all the time."

One day after school Wally saw a group of children playing baseball on the school field. Excitedly he went over to join them. He grabbed the bat from Freddy saying, "I'll show you how to really hit a ball."

"Hey you can't barge in like that, we're in the middle of a game," said Freddy. "Besides you can't play, you haven't practiced, you can't even catch a ball."

His friend Big Red teased, "Yeah, you can't even stand still; you jump around all the time, you don't pay attention - you're just like a monkey!"

4

Wally began to feel himself getting tense; his heart began to speed up, sweat broke out on his forehead, his head started aching, he felt like he was filling up like a balloon - his muscles felt so tight that he thought he would explode out of his skin! Suddenly his mind went numb and his body took over. He took the bat and threw it wildly hitting Big Red in the leg.

Wally stormed home. He kicked his books on the floor.

"Please put your books away," said his mother.

"No!" he yelled.

Wally was sent to his room. He slammed the door and threw his baseball cards on the floor.

6

A little later Tiny Turtle knocked at his bedroom door to ask if Wally wanted to go roller-blading. Wally pouted saying, "I don't want to do anything."

"What's the matter?" asked Tiny.

Wally explained what happened.

"I know how you feel," replied Tiny. "I've been teased too, but you can't lose control when someone teases you. If you do, they might even tease you more! You know, I learned a secret from Tommy Turtle. I'll tell it to you because it really happened to me."

"One day I was sitting in my room thinking, "I would rather stay home and watch TV. I don't want to go to school and write words - it's too hard. I can't do it. Besides I don't like the kids at school. They pick on me and tease me because I go so slowly. So I tease them and even try to hit them. Sometimes I sneak their pencils under my shell. Well, every day I told myself I wouldn't get into trouble but it was just too hard to remember not to get in trouble. I kept getting angry because the other kids were mean to me. I began to feel I was a bad turtle."

"Yes, that's exactly how I feel," said Wally.

"Well, I knew my solutions didn't have very good consequences because I felt bad and everyone was mad at me, even the teachers and my parents. So one day after a lot of thinking I came up with one solution. At first I was so angry I couldn't think of any solutions. Finally I decided to ask Tommy Turtle what to do. Now Tommy is not a Ninja turtle but he is the oldest wisest turtle in town. He is 200 years old and very kind and I thought he might be able to help, after all, he had survived a long time. Well I was really scared to tell him my problem but I got up my courage and told him."

"I'll tell you a secret Tiny," said Tommy, "you already have the answer to your problem with you. You have it everywhere you go."

"At first I didn't understand," said Tiny.

"It's your shell."

"My shell? I was even more confused."

Then Tommy said, "that's why you have a shell, so whenever you feel angry or upset, you can go in your shell. When you go in your shell you can rest for a minute, you can tell yourself to say, "stop, take three breaths, and calm down. Try to think of a happy place in your mind. See like this." Then Tommy showed me how he calmed down in his shell.

"Well, I figured Tommy's idea was worth a try. Sure enough, Wally, the next day someone was teasing me about how slow I was at writing. I started to get angry and almost hit him but I remembered what Tommy said and I stopped, went in my shell, took three breaths and told myself I could calm down. You know it was really comfy in my shell and soon I felt calm again. You know what else the teacher said? She said she was proud of me and that made me feel good."

"But you're lucky," Wally said, "I don't have a shell like you do!"

"Oh," said Tiny, "but you do. You can use an imaginary shell to keep control of your feelings. These days I don't even have to go inside my real shell. I use my pretend shell and the other kids don't even know I'm using it. They seem impressed that I'm so strong. You know, Tommy said he was in a race once with a hare and to everyone's surprise he beat the hare. He said it was because he used his shell to stay calm and then he just kept going."

"Wow!" said Wally, "that is powerful stuff. It is kind of like having a feelings shield; protecting you and keeping your feelings from jumping out of your body. I'll try to use it."

And so the next day when Wally saw the same group of
children playing baseball he approached them slowly - wearing
his imaginary shield. He waited before barging into the group
and watched them playing. After awhile he said to Big Red,
"You're pretty good at baseball! Can I play?"

"No way! You're reckless and dangerous."

Wally waited in his shell and told himself, "I can calm
down, I can handle this, I'm strong. I can try a solution." He
tried again, "I'm sorry Big Red, I wanted to play so much I lost
control of my feelings, but I won't make that mistake again."

Well, said Big Red reluctantly, "you can play if you stay in
the outfield I guess."

Wally wasn't exactly happy with this solution but he walked out into the field wearing his imaginary shield. He thought to himself, "I can handle this. At least I'm part of the team." Suddenly he felt calm and started to smile to himself, "Wait until I tell Tiny Turtle about my 'turtle power'!"

Questions for teachers or parents to ask their children while they are reading this book

1. What feelings did Wally have about baseball? Have you ever felt this way about something?

2. What was the problem with the way Wally approached the kids playing baseball the first time?

3. How did Wally know he had a problem?

4. How did he handle his feelings at first? What did you think about his solution to throw the bat? (Was it safe? Was it fair? Did it lead to good feelings?) What other solutions might he have chosen?

5. What did Tiny learn from Tommy about controlling his angry feelings? How did it work for Wally?

6. Why was Tiny a good friend? What did he do that was friendly?

7. What did Wally learn about himself?

8. What did he do differently the second time when he approached the other kids playing baseball?

9. Was Wally's solution to go to the outfield a good one? Why? Was it safe? Was it fair? Did it lead to good feelings?

10. How can Wally become a good team member?

CENSUS RETURNS
1841 - 1891
IN MICROFORM
A DIRECTORY TO LOCAL HOLDINGS
IN GREAT BRITAIN;
Channel Islands; Isle of Man

Jeremy Gibson and Elizabeth Hampson

SIXTH EDITION

Federation of Family History Societies

First published 1979 under the tiitle
Census Returns 1841 1851 1861 1871 on Microfilm by the
Federation of Family History Societies.

Sixth edition, updated reprint, published 1997 by
Federation of Family History Society (Publications) Ltd.,
2-4 Killer Street, Ramsbottom, Bury, Lancs. BL0 9BZ, England.

Second edition, 1980.
Third edition, 1981.
Fourth edition, as *Census Returns 1841-1881 on Microfilm*, 1982.
Fifth edition, 1988, reprinted 1990.

Sixth edition, as *Census Returns 1841-1891 in Microform*, 1994, updated reprint, 1997.

Sixth edition © J.S.W. Gibson 1994, 1997.

ISBN 1 872094 88 0

Cover illustration: Filling up the census paper. *Wife of his Bosom.* "Upon my word, Mr. Peewitt! Is this the Way you Fill up your Census? So you call Yourself the 'Head of the Family' - do you - and me a 'Female!' " (*Punch*, vol. 20, 1851, reproduced in *People Count*, Muriel Nissel, 1987).

Typeset from computer disks prepared by Jeremy Gibson and Elizabeth Hampson.
Printed by Parchment (Oxford) Limited.

ACKNOWLEDGMENTS

This sixth edition is based on the replies to a letter to libraries and record offices circulated earlier in 1994. As always we are deeply grateful to all those librarians and archivists who took time and trouble answering our enquiries. In this updated reprint minor addtions and alterations have been made as the result either of information from archivists and others, or of changes in nomenclature to repositories.

Scotland was included for the first time in the fifth edition. It is gratifying that census microfilm/fiche is now available in many more Scottish repositories, and that a Guide to these, *Genealogical microform holdings in Scottish Libraries*, by Margaret Nikolic, published in 1992, already is going into a second edition.

This is the second of the Guides in this series in which Elizabeth Hampson appears as co-editor. She has in fact done virtually all the work of preparing this new edition, circulating repositories, collating the replies and preparing the initial computer disc - but for her publication would have been long delayed.

J.S.W.G.

Federation of Family History Societies Publications Ltd. is a wholly owned subsidiary of
the Federation of Family History Societies, Registered Charity No. 1038721.

PREFACE

The original books of enumerators' returns for the censuses of 1841, 1851, 1861, 1871, 1881 and 1891, for England, Wales, the Channel Islands and the Isle of Man, are at the Public Record Office at Kew. Those for Scotland are at the General Register Office for Scotland, in Edinburgh.

These census records have attracted ever-growing attention from social, local and family historians. To prevent their physical deterioration they were, some time ago, filmed, and it is these microfilms or microfiche which visitors to the recently established Family Records Centre now consult. This is conveniently situated in central London, at 1 Myddelton Street, Islington EC1R 1UN. Entrance is free and no reader's ticket is necessary. For further information consult *Basic Facts about Using the Family Records Centre*, by Audrey Collins, FFHS, 1997. The G.R.O. for Scotland is just off Princes Street, adjacent to the Scottish Record Office. Here there is a modest daily charge.

The existence of such microfilm and fiche has made it possible for libraries and record offices throughout the country to acquire copy films for their own areas, usually for all of the six census years open to the public under the '100 years rule'. This Directory shows the extent to which they have done so.

There now appears to be virtually complete local coverage of all census years throughout Great Britain. It should be emphasised that the information given depends much on the detail supplied by the library or record office concerned, qualified by the limitations of space. The census was organised in Registration Districts (RDs), based on Poor Law Unions, and Sub-Districts (SDs), often overlapping county boundaries. Thus straight-forward seeming 'complete county' entries may hide missing places on county borders, or include those in neighbouring counties. More specific information on these is always welcome. The hinterland of towns respects no boundaries, and their library holdings are often complex and intermingling. Modern holdings may be for present administrative areas, different both from the pre-1974 counties and the nineteenth century census districts.

Nearly all holdings 1841 to 1881 are on microfilm, or for 1891 on microfiche (earlier years are becoming available on fiche also); but where photocopies are held they are shown. Some transcripts also are listed, but transcription is now increasing to such an extent that their inclusion is discretionary. An even more useful growth field is in indexing, usually for 1851, and the publication of such indexes. Surnames indexes have now been published for many counties, sometimes backed by transcripts. Such is their proliferation and rate of appearance in published form that details of them must be confined to the companion Guide in this Series, *Marriage, Census and Other Indexes for Family Historians*. This is updated regularly so can include more recent developments than this Directory may.

Two of the Guides in this series which have appeared since the fifth edition was published in 1988 (updated 1990) are of relevance. *Local Census Listings: 1522-1930* (with Mervyn Medlycott, 1992, 3rd edition 1997) covers all such pre-1841 in great detail, so the previous occasional references to these have been omitted in this edition. Part 4 of *Poor Law Union Records* (with Frederic A. Youngs, jr., 1997) is a *Gazetteer of England and Wales*, showing which places constituted each Union, often overlapping county boundaries. As the census registration districts were based on the unions, this can help to identify in which registration district or sub-district a place may have been.

The most significant recent development has been the transcription and indexing, by county, of the 1881 census for the whole country, initiated and funded by the Church of Jesus Christ of Latter Day Saints (Mormons). Family History societies have in large part contributed the voluntary labour for much of this gigantic undertaking. The results have been made available on microfiche, and are widely available both through the societies and at repositories. Some of these county fiche are listed, but on no systematic basis, so enquiry should always be made.

Several useful publications about the census have appeared since the last edition of this Directory. For guidance on the content and interpretation of the various censuses, readers are recommended to two by Sue Lumas, *An Introduction to The Census Returns of England and Wales* (F.F.H.S., 1992) and *Making Use of the Census* (P.R.O. Guide No. 1, 2nd edition 1993); and Edward Higgs' authoritative survey, *Making Sense of the Census: The Manuscript Returns for England and Wales, 1801-1901* (H.M.S.O. for the Public Record Office, 1989). Also of interest is *People Count: A history of the General Register Office,* by Muriel Nissel (H.M.S.O. for the Office of Population Censuses and Surveys, 1987).

Holdings at public libraries and record offices are normally available to the public without restriction (though in at least one local record office a daily charge is now made). However, as use of a microfilm or fiche reader will be necessary, it is always advisable to make a prior appointment; and at the same time check that the information in this Guide is correct.

Holdings at universities and colleges are included for information, but are not necessarily open to the public, being the private property of the institutions concerned. Access to them, if granted at all, is a privilege which should be accepted with gratitude, and not taken as a right. Their custodians have their first duty to their own staff and students, and may well decline to allow access to the public.

Constructive criticism and correction of errors are always very welcome. No compiler can pretend to a detailed knowledge of the whole country. We are of course always glad to hear of new or extended holdings, and to receive suggestions for improving entries for existing ones. These should be sent to Jeremy Gibson at the address below.

Our sympathy went out to the librarian who commented on one of our circulars, "Haven't (because of sheer bloody pressure of work) yet managed to look at all the reels supplied." Maybe users of this Guide, with the odd moment to spare, can help to relieve that pressure!

J.S.W.G. and E.H.
Harts Cottage,
Church Hanborough,
Witney, Oxon. OX8 8AB.

BEDFORDSHIRE

Census Indexes and Publications:
Bedfordshire, 1851: see *Marriage, Census and Other Indexes* for Bedfordshire FHS published index and search service to whole county, 1851.
Ecclesiastical Census, 1851, ed. D.W. Busby, Beds. Record Soc. **54**, 1975.

Bedfordshire Record Office, Bedford.
41-91: whole county.

Bedford Central Library.
41-91: whole county.

Luton Central Library.
41-91: Barton, Biscot, W Hyde, Leagrave, Limbury, **Luton**, Streatley, Sundon; also Caddington 91; Clophill 41; Dunstable 51 & 91; Flitton 41; Lr and Upr Gravenhurst 41; Haynes 41; High Gobion 41; Houghton Regis 51 & 91; Humbershoe 51; E Hyde 41,61,71 & 91; Kensworth 51 & 91; Manstead 51; Markyate 51-71 & 91; New Mill End 51; Pulloxhill 41; Round Green 91; Sharpenhoe 51; Shillington 41; Silshoe 41; Stopsley 51-71 & 91; Studham 51 & 91; Tottenhoe 51 & 91; Whipsnade 51 & 91.

County Reference Library, Aylesbury.
41-91: some parishes in Leighton Buzzard area bordering Buckinghamshire.

Milton Keynes Library.
41-91: some parishes in Leighton Buzzard area bordering Buckinghamshire.

Cambridgeshire Record Office, Cambridge.
61,71: Little Barford.
81: Mormon Index for the county.
Indexes 51: Arlesey, Blunham, Everton, Henlow, Kimbolton, Potton, Sandy and St. Neots districts.

County Record Office, Huntingdon.
41: Gt. Barford, Bolnhurst, Clapham, Colmworth, Dean, Goldington, Keysoe, Knotting Melchbourne, Milton Ernest, Oakley, Ravensden, Renhold, Riseley, Roxton, Wilden, Yeldon.
41-91: Swineshead, 51,61,81; 41-61,81-91 Eaton Socon, Dean, Pertenhall, Shelton, Little Staughton, Tilbrook.
51-91: Little Barford.
Transcripts: 51 indexed transcripts for parishes in St Neots district. Beds. FHS surname index for area adjoining Hunts; 81 Mormon microfiche.

Northamptonshire Record Office.
51,71,81: Farndish, Hinwick, Poddington, Wymington.

BERKSHIRE

North-west part now in Oxfordshire.

Census Indexes and Publications:
Berkshire, 1851: see *Marriage, Census and Other Indexes* for details of Berkshire FHS county index project and published sections.

Berkshire County Library.
Libraries at *Slough, Maidenhead, Windsor, Bracknell* and *Newbury* have **41-91** for their local areas. *Ascot Durning* has **41-81** for Ascot only (incomplete).

County Local Studies Library, Reading.
41-91: whole of pre 1974 **Berkshire**.

Berkshire Record Office, Reading.
41: Beech Hill (Basingstoke RD).
51: Reading (all 3 ancient parishes) with index to families, places, streets in progress.
51: Ashbury; Bourton; Buckland; Buscot; Coleshill; Compton Beauchamp; Gt Coxwell; Eaton Hastings; Lit Faringdon; Fernham; Hinton Waldrist; Langford; Longcot; Pusey; Shrivenham; Stanford in the Vale (part of); Watchfield; Woolstone.

Bulmershe College of Higher Education, Earley, Reading.
41-71: Reading.

Centre for Oxon Studies, Oxford Central Library.
91: Complete county.
41-81: All N-W of county (Vale of White Horse, incl. Abingdon, Faringdon, Wallingford, Wantage; now in Oxon.).
Also Aldermaston 41-71; Aldworth 41-71; Ashampstead 41-81; Avington 41; Basildon 41-81; Beedon 51-71; Beenham 41-71; Blagrove 41; Bockhampton 41; Bradfield 41-81; Brightwalton 51-71; Bucklebury 41-81; Bucklebury Alley 51,61; Burghfield 41-71; Caversham (formerly Oxon) 41-81; Chaddleworth 41-71; Clewer 41; Eastbury 41; Easthampstead 41; Enborne 41; Englefield 41-81; Farnborough 41-71; Grazeley 41,61; Greenham 41; Hadley 41; Hampstead Marshall 41; Hampstead Norris 51-71; E Hanney 41-81; Hermitage 41; Hungerford 41; Lit Hungerford 51-71; E and W Ilsley 41-71; Inkpen 41; Kintbury 41; Lambourn 41; Langford 41-81; Midgham 41; Mortimer 51-71; Newtown 41; Padworth 41-71; Pangbourne 41-81; Peasemore 51-71; Purley 41-81; Remenham 51-81; Shaw cum Donnington 41; E and W Shefford 41; Shinfield 41; Speen 41; Stanford Dingley 41-81; Stratfield Mortimer 41-71; Streatley 41-81; Sulham 41-81; Sulhampstead Abbots and Banister 41-71; Thatcham 41; Theale 81; Tidmarsh 41-81; Tilehurst 41-81; Waltham St. Lawrence 41; Warfield 41; Wragrave 41; Wasing 41; Welford 41; Wellhouse 51-71; Windsor and Old Windsor 41; Winkfield 41; Wokefield 41-71; Wokingham Union 41; W Woodhay 41; Woolhampton 41; Wooley Green 71; Yattendon 41-81.

Berkshire continued

Abingdon Library (Oxon C.C.).
51-91: Abingdon RD: SDs of Abingdon, Cumnor, Fifield, Nuneham and Sutton Courtenay.

Gloucestershire Record Office, Gloucester.
51: Buckland; Hinton Waldrist; Longcot; Pusey; Stanford in the Vale.

Surrey Record Office, Woking (from mid-1998). Clewer 51; Dedworth 51; Sunningdale 51,61; Sunninghill 51-81; New Windsor 51; Old Windsor 51-81; Windsor Castle 51.

Wiltshire Record Office, Trowbridge.
Avington 51-81; E Garston 51,61,81; Hungerford 51-81; Inkpen 51-81; Kintbury 51-81; Lambourne 51-81; E and W Shefford 51,81; Shinfield 41; Swallowfield 41; Wokingham 41; W Woodhay 51-81.

BUCKINGHAMSHIRE
Southern tip now in Berkshire.

Census Indexes and Publications:
See *Marriage, Census and Other Indexes* for Buckinghamshire FHS projects.
Buckinghamshire Returns of the Census of Religious Worship 1851, ed. Edward Legg, Bucks Record Soc. **27**, 1991.

Buckinghamshire County Reference Library (Buckinghamshire Collection), Aylesbury;
duplicates at *Milton Keynes Library.*
41-91: complete county. 51: census index (BFHS) on computer.

High Wycombe Library.
41-91: southern half of county only.

Chesham Library.
41-91: Amersham and Chesham areas only.

Buckingham Library.
41-91: Buckingham area only.

Slough Central Library.
41-91: Burnham; Colnbrook (part); Datchet; Dorney; Eton; Eton Wick; Farnham Royal; Fulmer; Hedgerley; Hitcham; Horton; Iver; Langley Marish; Slough; Stoke Poges; Taplow, Upton-cum-Chalvey; Wexham; Wraysbury.
41-81: New Windsor and Old Windsor.

Bedfordshire Record Office, Bedford.
Cheddington 51-91; Edlesborough 51-91; Grove 51,61, 91; Ivinghoe 51-91; Linslade 51-91; Mentmore 51-91; Slapton 51-91; Soulbury 51-91; Stoke Hammond 51-91; Wing 51-91.

Berkshire Record Office, Reading.
51,91: Fawley, Hambleden, Medmenham
91: Frieth.

Northamptonshire Record Office.
51,71,81: Biddlesden; Calverton (not 71); Stony Stratford (not 71); Turweston; Westbury; Wolverton.

Buckinghamshire continued

Centre for Oxon. Studies, Oxford Central Library.
91: Complete county.
Addington 71; Bledlow 81; Boarstall 51-71; Boycott 41,51; Bradenham 81; Brill 51-81; Chilton 41-81; Long Crendon 51-81; Dorton 51-81; Fawley 81; Fingest 51,81; Hambleden 51-81; Horsenden 81; Hughenden 81; Ibstone 41,51,81; Ickford 51-81; Ilmer 81; Kingsey 41-71; Lillingstone Lovell 41,51; Medmenham 41,71,81; Lit Missenden 81; Oakley 51-81; Princes Risborough 81; Radnage 81; Remenham 81; Saunderton 81; Shabbington 51-81; Stokenchurch (formerly Oxon) 41-81; Worminghall 51-81; W Wycombe 81.

Henley Library (Oxon C.C.).
51-91: Henley RD: SDs of Henley and Watlington; probably incl. Medmenham, Remenham, Hambleden, Fawley.

CAMBRIDGESHIRE

See *Genealogical Sources in Cambridgeshire*, Cambs RO, second edition, 1994, for exact location of 41-91 census mf for all Cambs. parishes.

Census Indexes and Publications:
Cambridgeshire and the Isle of Ely, 1851: See *Marriage, Census and Other Indexes* for details of Cambridgeshire FHS published index and search service, complete county transcribed and indexed.

Cambridgeshire Record Office, Cambridge.
41-91: Cambridgeshire and the Isle of Ely
(51 excl. Snailwell, Landwade, Burwell, Ashley, Kennett, which are lost;
61 excl. Ely (except detached part and Westmoor), Tydd St. Giles, Whaddon (last 4 pages), Stapleford (last 2 pages), Cambridge St. Andrew the Less (20 pages) and St. Michael (last 3 pages), which are lost).
Note. The Office holds censearch index to **1841** county census; also transcripts and indexes for **1851** for the complete historic county and the Isle of Ely, compiled by the Cambridgeshire FHS; also the Mormon 1881 indexes on fiche.

County Record Office, Huntingdon.
41,61: Arrington, Barrington, Barton, Comberton, Coton, Cottenham, Grantchester, Harlton, Haslingfield, Orwell, Shepreth, Wimpole.
51-61, 91: Papworth Agnes. Boxworth, Conington, Croxton, Croydon, Fen Drayton, Lt Gransden, Lolworth, Over, Papworth Agnes, Swavesey.
61: Cambridgeshire and the Isle of Ely, excl. Ely (except detached part and Westmoor), Tydd St. James, Whaddon (last 4 pages), which are lost.
51-71, 91: Graveley and Thorney.
Transcripts and Indexes **41-81:** Whittlesey,
51: Caxton district, Swavesey sub-district, Thorney, Wisbech St. Peter.
81: Mormon Surname Index for all county.

Cambridgeshire continued

Wisbech Library.
41-91: Isle of Ely complete.

Wisbech Teachers' Centre.
Wisbech 41-91.

Northamptonshire Record Office.
Thorney 81.

Peterborough Central Library.
Thorney 41-51, 91.

Suffolk Record Office, Bury St. Edmunds.
51-91: Cambs. parishes bordering Suffolk.

Bedfordshire Record Office.
51: Arrington, Barton, Bourn, Caldecote, Caxton, Cherry Hinton, Chesterton, Childerley, Comberton, Coton, Cottenham, Croydon cum Clapton, Croxton, Dry Drayton, Elsworth, Eltisley, Lit Eversden, Fen Ditton, Fulbourn, Gamlingay, Girton, Lit Gransden, Grantchester, Hardwick, Harlton, Harston, Haslingfield, Hatley St. George, E Hatley, Hauxton, Histon, Horningsea, Impington, Kingston, Knapwell, Landbeach, Long Stowe, Longstanton St. Michael and All SS, Madingley, Milton, Newton, Oakington, Orwell, Papworth St. Agnes and St. Everard, Rampton, Gt and Lit Shelford, Stapleford, Stow cum Quy, Tadlow, Teversham, Toft, Trumpington, Waterbeach, Gt and Lit Wilbraham, Willingham, Wimpole.

Hertfordshire Local Studies Library, Hertford.
41-91: an area of S.W. Cambs incl Melbourn R.D.

Saffron Walden Library (Essex).
Gt and Lit Abington 51-91; Balsham 51-81; Bartlow 51-91; Castle Camps 51-71; Duxford 51,61,81,91; Hildersham 51-91; Hinxton 51,61,81,91; Horseheath 51,61,81; Ickleton 51,61,81,91; Linton 51-91; Pampisford 51,61,81,91; Sawston 51,61,81,91; Shudy Camps 51-91; Whittlesford 51,61,81,91.

CHESHIRE
Northern border now in Greater Manchester; Wirral now in Merseyside.

See Cheshire *Censuses of 1841, 1851, 1861, 1871 and 1881*, D.H. Way, now out of print but most local Cheshire libraries have reference copies. This gives exact PRO refs. for all Cheshire places, location of microfilms, and on page 15 lists surname indexes, all 1851, as available in 1984.

Census Indexes and Publications:
See *Marriage, Census and Other Indexes* for 1851 census index publications and projects of the FHS of Cheshire, the North Cheshire FHS and the Warrington Group of the Liverpool & District FHS.

Cheshire continued

Cheshire Record Office, Chester.
41-91: complete historic county.

Chester City Record Office.
41-91: Chester and neighbouring villages and townships.
Cheshire Libraries and Museums Dept.
41-91: complete pre and post-1974 **county** (excl. Alsager/Sandbach district). Each local area is held at the local library: *Alsager, Chester, Congleton, Crewe, Ellesmere Port, Knutsford, Macclesfield, Nantwich, Neston, Northwich, Poynton, Runcorn (Shopping City), Sandbach, Warrington, Widnes, Wilmslow, Winsford.*
Pre-1974 areas at *Ellesmere Port* (for Wirral) and *Macclesfield* (former eastern border).

Birkenhead Central Library (Information Services, Wirral Archives).
41-91: Wirral Hundred (including Birkenhead, Wallasey, Bebington, Neston, Ellesmere Port, Heswall and Hoylake). This includes the current county district of South Wirral as well as the area of the Metropolitan Borough of Wirral.

Stockport Central Library.
41-91 unless shown otherwise: Adlington, Ches.; Altrincham 51; Ashley 51; Ashton upon Mersey 51; Baguley 51; Bollin Fee 51; Bollington 51, 91; Bosden 51; Bowden 51; Bramhall; Bredbury; Brinnington; Butley; Cheadle Bulkeley; Cheadle Hulme 51-61,81-91; Cheadle Moseley; Compstall 51, 91; Disley 41-71, 91; Dukinfield 41,71; Dunham Massey 51; Fallibroome 91; Fulshaw 51; Gatley; Gee Cross 51, 91; Godley 51, 91; Hale; Handforth; Hazel Grove; Heaton Norris; Hurdsfield 51, 91; Hyde; Lyme Handley 51, 91; Marple; Mellor; Middlewood 51, 91; Mobberley 51; Mottram St. Andrew 41-61,71, 91; Newton-in-Werneth 71-91; Newton, Prestbury 91; Norbury; Northenden 51; Offerton; Poii Shrigley 51, 91; Pownall Fee 51; Poynton; Prestbury; Reddish; Romiley; Sale 51; Stockport; Stockport Etchells; Styal 51; Timperley 51; Torkington; Tytherington 51,91; Upton 51, 91; Werneth; Whitfield 51; Whitle 41-71; Woodford; Worth 41,51.
See *Genealogy in Stockport: A Guide to Sources...*, Handlist **14**, 1994 (£2.00).

Manchester Central Library (Local Hist.).
Altrincham 41,51,71,81; Ashley 41-81; Ashton-upon-Mersey 41-81; Bollin Fee 51,71,81; Bollington 41; Bowdon 41-81; Carrington 41; Cheadle 71; Dunham Massey 41-81; Edgeley 71; Fulshaw 51; Godley 71; Hale 41,51,71,81; Heaton Norris 41; Mobberley 51-81; Newton 71; Partington 41; Pownall Fee 51-81; Sale 41,51,71,81; Stockport (pt) 71; Styal 51-81; Timperley 41,51; Wilmslow 51-81.

Cheshire continued

Stalybridge Library (Tameside M.B.).
41-91: Broadbottom, Dukinfield, Godley, Hollingworth, Hyde, Micklehurst, Mottram-in-Longendale, Newton, Stalybridge.

Trafford Local Studies Centre, Sale Library.
(Some of the following places are now in Greater Manchester.)
41: Clifton; Gilda Brook; Levenshulme; Moss Brow; Moss Side; Moston; Newton Heath; Openshaw; Park Gate; Pendlebury; Pendleton; Reddish; Roe Green; Rusholme; Warburton (& 91); Warburton's Cross; Withington; Winton, Worsley.
51: Aston by Budworth; Budworth; Knutsford; Lymm (& 71); Millington (& 81); Mobberley; Monton (and 61); Northern Etchells; Northenden; Ollerton; Peover; Pickmere; Plumley; Pownall Fee; Tabley; Toft; Wilmslow; Winton (& 71).
41-91: Altrincham; Ashley (not 61,71); Ashton-upon-Mersey (not 71); Baguley (not 71,81,); Barton-upon-Irwell (not 71,91); Bollington (not 61,91); Bowden (not 71,81); Carrington (not 61); Daveyhulme (not 81); Dumplington 41-71; Flixton; Hale; Lostock 41-71; Stretford; Timperely; Urmston; Sale.
61: Vessels on the Irwell & Bridgewater Canal; Whalley Range; Whittleswick.
71: Budworth; Eccles.
51-71: Bromyhurst; Croft ('s Bank) & 41; Sale; Traffford Park.
51,61,91: Irlam.
51-71,91: Cadishead.
71,91: Partington.
81: Agden; High Legh.
81,91: Old Trafford.
91: Alworkhouse; Barton Workhouse; Blind Asylum; Canal Boats; Deaf and Dumb School; Manchester; Patricroft; Stretford.

Derbyshire County Library, Matlock.
Disley 41-91; Furness Vale 41-91; Hattersley 41, 51, 81, 91; Hollingworth 41-91; Macclesfield 51, 91; Macclesfield Forest 41-91; Marple 41-81; Matley 41, 51, 71; Mellor 41-91; Micklehurst 41-81; Mottram 41, 51, 81, 91; Rainow 51-91; Stayley 41-81; Stalybridge 41-71; Stockport 61; Taxal 41-91; Yeardsley cum Whaley 41-91.

Derby Central Library, Local Studies Dept.
Disley 51-91; Fishpool 91; Hattersley 91; Hollingworth 91; Kettleshulme 91; Macclesfield 91; Marple 61; Mellor 41-91; Mottram 91; Norton 91; Rainow 91; Stockport; Sutton (nr. Macclesfield) 91; Winde (nr. Macclesfield) 91.

Staffordshire Record Office.
61: Astbury, Moreton cum Alcomlow, Newbold, Somerford Booths (also 41).
71,81: Tittenley.

Newcastle-under-Lyme Library.
81: Basford.

Flintshire Record Office, Hawarden.
51-91: a few Cheshire parishes bordering Flintshire and Denbighshire (including Chester city).

Denbighshire Record Office, Ruthin.
51,71-91: a few parishes bordering Denbighshire.

CORNWALL

Census Indexes:
   Cornwall 1881: see *Marriage, Census and Other Indexes* for Cornwall FHS project.

Cornish Studies Library, Redruth.
41-91: Complete county; index to 1881 also held.

Cornwall County Record Office, Truro.
41-71: complete county.
(In great use, prior appointment essential.) Mormon transcript and index of the **1881** census held.

Westcountry Studies Library (Devon Library Services), Castle Street, Exeter.
Maker 41, Sheviock 61, St. Stephen by Launceston 81, St. Thomas the Apostle 81.
41-91: Boyton.
51-91: Egloskerry, Tamerton, Tremaine, Treneglos, Tresmeer, Warbstow.
61-91: Calstock.

CUMBERLAND
Now part of Cumbria.

Census Indexes and Publications:
See *Marriage, Census and Other Indexes* for South Cumberland Index 1851 (at Cumbria RO, Carlisle and Barrow) and Cumbria FHS 1851 published indexes and search service.

Carlisle, Whitehaven and Workington Libraries (Cumbria County Library).
41-91: Whole county and Carlisle holds an index by place, including a street index to Carlisle. Personal name index at Carlisle for 1881.

Penrith Library.
91: Index for parts of Cumberland and part of Westmorland.

Cumbria Record Office, Carlisle.
41: Cumberland.
51: Alston, Austhwaite, Birker, Bootle Workhouse, Brampton, Eskdale, Greystoke, Hayton, Hesket New Market, Ireby, Irton, Mungrisdale, Netherwasdale, Penrith Workhouse, Talkin, Threlkeld, Ulpha, Wasdale, Whitehaven Holy Trinity, Whitehaven Workhouse (all transcripts except Brampton).
71: Cumberland and Westmorland names in parishes now in Cleveland.

Cumberland continued

Cumbria Record Office, Barrow-in-Furness.
Transcripts: **41-91;** South-West Cumberland
(Millom, Bootle, Waberthwaite and surrounding
villages).

Cumbria Record Office, Kendal.
51: Hutton, Watermillock.

DERBYSHIRE

Census Indexes and Publications:
    *The Derbyshire Returns to the 1851 Religious
Census,* ed. Margery Tranter. 1995. Derbys. R.S.
    Derbyshire 1851: See *Marriage, Census and
Other Indexes* for Derbyshire FHS census index
publications and search services.

Derbyshire County Library, Matlock.
41-91: complete county (except for Walton on
Trent 1841 which is missing at the P.R.O.)
Index of places; Street index for Derby 41-91.

*Derby Central Library (Local Studies Dept.),
25b Irongate, Derby.*
41-91: complete county (minus Walton on Trent as
above).
Index of places in county 41-81;
Street index for Derby 41-91;
Surname index, Derby only 51.

Nottingham University Library.
41-91: complete county.

Ilkeston Library.
41-81: Ilkeston and adjacent villages

Chesterfield Library.
41-91: North Derbyshire (excl. Glossop).
(**91** all North and Mid Derbyshire as far south as
Ashbourne, Belper and Ilkeston).

Glossop Library.
41-91: parish of Glossop.

Buxton Library.
41-91: Buxton and adjacent villages.

Belper Library.
61-91: Belper and adjacent villages.

Long Eaton Library.
91: Long Eaton and adjacent villages.

Ripley Library.
41-61, 81-91: Ripley and adjacent villages.

Swadlincote Library.
91: Swadlincote and adjacent villages.

Derbyshire continued

New Mills Library.
41-91: New Mills and adjacent villages.

*Nottinghamshire Local Studies Library; and
Nottinghamshire Archives, Nottingham.*
51: Basford RD: Codnor and Loscoe, Codnor Park,
Heanor, Shipley, Ilkeston; **Mansfield RD:** Pleasley,
Ault Hucknall, Glapwell, Upper Langwith, Scarcliffe,
Tibshelf, Blackwell, S Normanton, Pinxton;
Worksop RD: Whitwell, Barlborough, Clowne,
Elmton.
81: Aldercar, Astwith, Ault Hucknall, Barlborough,
Blackwell, Clowne, Codnor, Codnor Park,
Cotmanhay, Cresswell, Elmton, Clapwell, Hallam
Fields, Lit Hallam, Hardstoft, Hardwick, Heanor,
Ilkeston, Langley, Langley Mill, Upr Langwith,
Loscoe, Loscoe Grange, Marlpool, New Houghton,
S Normanton, Palterton, Pleasley, Pleasley Vale,
Upr Pleasley, Rowthorne, Scarcliffe, Shipley,
Shirebrook, Stainsby, Stoneyford, Stoney Houghton,
Stuffynwood, Tibshelf, Warsop Park, Whitwell,
Wood End, Wood Lincoln.
41,61,71: parishes bordering Notts.

Sutton-in-Ashfield (Notts.) Central Library.
Ault Hucknall 51-91; Astwith 61-91; Bagthorpe 51-
91; Begarlee 51; Blackwell 51-91; Brinsley 51-91;
Codnor and Loscoe 51-71,91; Glapwell 51-91;
Hardstoft 61-81; Hardwick 81; Ironville 51;
Kimberley 51; Upr Langwith 51-81; Mansfield
Woodhouse 61-91; Moorgreen 51,71,81; New
Houghton 61,81,91; Newthorpe 51-91; S
Normanton 51-91; Palterton 51-91; Pinxton 51-91;
Pleasley 51-91; Rowthorne 71-91; Scarcliffe 51-91;
Shirebrook 61-91; Stainsby 61-91; Stoney
Houghton 61-91; Tibshelf 51-91; Underwood 51-91;
Wassop 61-91; Watnall Cantelupe 51; Watnall
Chaworth 51.

Mansfield (Notts.) Central Library.
Aldecar Row 71; Astwith 71,81; Ault Hucknall 51-81;
Bagthorpe 61,71; Barlborough 61,71; Belph 71;
Belph Moor 71; Blackwell 51; Clowne 61-81;
Codnor 61-81; Cresswell 41,71,81; Cresswell Crags
71; Elmton 61-81; Glapwell 51-81; Golden Valley
71,81; Hardstoft 71,81; Hardwick 71,81; Houghton
61; Ironville 71; Loscoe 61-81; Loscoe Grange 81; S
Normanton 51; Palterton 71,81; Pinxton 51;
Pleasley 51-81; Pleasley Vale 81; Upr Pleasley 81;
Riley 71; Rowthorne 71,81; Scarcliffe 51-81;
Shirebrook 51-81; Stainsby 71,81; Standley 71;
Stanley 81; Stockley 71; Stony Houghton 71,81;
Stone Row 71; Stoneyford 71; Stuffynwood 81;
Tibshelf 51; Woodlinkin 71.

Stockport (Ches.) Central Library.
Bugsworth 41; Charlesworth 41,61,91; Chinley 41;
Chisworth 41,61,81; Chunal 51; Dinting 41-61;
Glossop 41-61,81-91; Hadfield 51; Hayfield
51,61,81,91; Ludworth 41-61,81,91; New Mills
51,71; Ollersett 51; Padfield 51; Rowarth 91;
Simmondly 51; Strines 91; Thornset 41-71.

Derbyshire continued

Sheffield Archives, 52 Shoreham Street.
Alfreton 41; Ashover 41; Barlborough 41,51;
Blackwell 41; Gt Barlow 51-71;; Beauchief 41-81;
Beighton 41-81; Bolsover 41; Brackenfield 41;
Brampton 41; Chesterfield (Workhouse) 71; Clowne
51; Coal Aston 41,51,71; Cutthorpe 41; Dore 41-81;
Dronfield 41,51,71; Duckmanton 51; Eckington
41-81; Elmton 41; Glapwell 41; High Lane 41-71;
Holmesfield 41,51,71; Inkersall 51,71; Killamarsh
41-71; Little Barlow 41,51; Mastin Moor 51,71;
Middle Hanley 51-71; Morton 41; Nether Handley
51-71; Pinxton 41; Pleasley 41; Renishaw 41-81;
Ridgeway 41-71; Speedwell 51,71; Spinkhill 41-81,
Springwell 51-71; Staveley 41,61,71;
Sutton-cum-Duckmanton 51; Totley 41-81; Troway
41-71; Unstone 41,51,71; Upper Langwith 41; West
Handley 51-71; Whitwell 51.

Staffordshire Record Office, Stafford.
Alkmonton 71; Alsop en le Dale 71; Ashbourne 71;
Atlow 71; Ballidon 71; Barton Blount 61-81;
Bearwardcote 51,81; Biggin 71; Bonsall 71;
Boylestone 51-81; Bradbourne 71; Bradley 71;
Brailsford 71; Brassington 71; Bretby 51,81; W
Broughton 51,71; Burnaston 51,81; Callow 71;
Carsington 71; Castle Gresley 51; Catton 51,81;
Caulwell 51,81; Church Broughton 51-81; Church
Gresley 51,81; Clifton 61-81; Cubley 51-81; Culland
71; Dalbury 51,81; Dale Botton 71; Doveridge
51-81; Drakelow 51-81; Edlaston 71; Ednaston 71;
Eggington 51-71; Etwall 51,81; Fenny Bentley
71,81; Findern 51,81; Foremark 51,81; Foston
51-81; Gatham 71; Harehill 51; Hartington 71;
Hatton 51-81; Heath Green 51,71; Hilton 51-81;
Hognaston 71; Hollington 71; Hoon 51-71; Hope 71;
Hopton 71; Hulland Ward 71; Hungry Bentley 71;
Ible 71; Ingleby 81; Kirk Ireton 71; Kniveton 71; Lea
Hall 71; Lees 51; Linton 51,81; Longford 71;
Mappleton 51,71,81; Marston on Dove 51-81;
Marston Montgomery 51,71,81; Mercaston 71;
Mickleover 51,81; Middleton 71; Milton 51,81; Muse
Lane 51; New Hall 51-81; Newton Grange 71;
Newton Solney 51,81; Norbury 51-71; Offcote 71;
Osleston 51-81; Osmaston 51; Parwich 71;
Radbourne 51,81; Repton 51,81; Rodsley 71;
Rosliston 51,81; Roston 51-71; Sapperton 51;
Scropton 51-81; Shirley 71; Snelston 61-81;
Somershall Herbert 51-71; Stapenhill 51; Stenson
51,81; Sturston 71; Stydd 71; Sudbury 51-81;
Sutton on the Hill 51-81; Swadlincote 51,81; Thorpe
71,81; Thurvaston 51-81; Tissington 71,81; Trusley
51,81; Twyford 51,81; Underwood 71; Walton on
Trent 51,81; Willington 51; Winkhill 71; Winshill
61,71; Wyaston 71; Yeaveley 71; Yeldersley 71.

Manchester Central Library.
Buxworth 41-61.

Leicestershire Record Office.
81: Castle Donington.
41-81: Leicestershire, which may include some
bordering Derbyshire parishes.

Burton-upon-Trent (Staffs.) Library.
Barton Blount 51,61,91; Boylestone 51-81; Bretby
41,51; Burnaston 51; Calke 41; Castle Gresley
41,51,61,71,91; Catton 41-91; Cauldwell 41,51,91;
Church Broughton 51,61,81,91; Church Gresley
41,51,91; Coton-in-the-Elms 41-71,91; Cubley
51-81; Dalbury Lees 51; Derby Hills 41; Doveridge
51-81; Drakelow 41,51,71; Draycott 41-81; Egginton
51,61,81,91; Etwall 51; Findern 51; Foremark 41,51;
Foston 51,61,71,91; Hartshorne 41; Hatton
51,61,81,91; Hilton 51,61,81,91; Hoon 51,61,91;
Ingleby 41,51; Linton 41,51,71,91; Linton Heath 71;
Lullington 41,51,71,91; Marston Montgomery 51-81;
Marston-on-Dove 51,61,91; Melbourne 41;
Mickleover 51; Milton 41,51; Newhall 41-61,91;
Newton Solney 41,51; Normanton 41; Osleston with
Thurvaston 51,61,81,91; Osmaston 41; Radbourne
51; Repton 41,51; Rosliston 41-61,81,91; Scropton
51,61,81,91; Shardlow 41; Smisby 41; Stanton
41-61; Stanton-by-Bridge 41; Sudbury 51-81;
Sutton-on-the-Hill 51,61,81,91; Swadlincote
41,51,91; Swarkeston 41; Trusley 51; Twyford 51;
Walton-on-Trent 51-81,91; Willington 51.

DEVON

Census Indexes and Publications:
    See *Marriage, Census and Other Indexes* for
details of Devon FHS published indexes, Plymouth
1851; and for Exeter 1851-1881 published indexes.
    Devon in The Religious Census of 1851. Ed. and
pub'd, 1990, by Michael J.L. Wickes (£10, from 2
Myra Court, Irsha St., Appledore, Bideford, Devon.

*Westcountry Studies Library, Devon Library
Services, Castle Street, Exeter.*
41-91: whole county.
Excl. **Dorset border:** Dalwood 41; Stockland 41.
Excluding **Somerset border:** Yarcombe 71.
Mormon Surname index to 81 census for N Devon.

Plymouth Central Library.
41-91: Plymouth, Devonport, Stonehouse, all
parishes (incl. Charles, St. Andrew, St. Budeaux,
Stoke Damarel). Some following may be 91 also.
Bere Ferrers 41,81; Bickleigh 51,61,81; Brixton
51,61,81; Buckland Monachorum 61,71,81;
Colebrook 71,81; Compton Gifford 51-81;
Cornwood 51-81; Eggbuckland 41-81; Ermington
51-81; Harford 51,61,81; Holbeton 51-81; Lifton 61;
Make 41,81; Meavy 41,81; Milton Abbot 61,
Modbury 61; Newton Ferrers 51-81; Pennycross
41,51,71,81; W.Peverell 61,81; Plympton St. Mary
41-81; Plympton St. Maurice 41-61,81; Plymstock
41-81; Revelstoke 41-61,81; Roborough 41,81;
Shaugh Prior 41-81; Tamerton Foliot 51-81;
Tavistock 61, Wembury 41-81; Yealmpton 41-81.

Devon continued

Plymouth Polytechnic.
51,71,81: Plymouth: Charles; St Andrew;
East Stonehouse; Devonport; Stoke Damarel.
51,71: Compton Gifford.
71 only: Brixton, Buckleigh, Cornwood,
Eggbuckland, Ermington, Harford, Holbeton, Laira
Green, Newton Ferrers, Pennycross, Plympton St.
Mary and St Maurice, Plymstock, Revelstoke, St.
Budeaux, Shaugh Prior, Tamerton Foliot, Wembury,
Yealmpton.

College of St Mark and St John, Plymouth.
51-71: Plymouth: Charles and St. Andrew.

Local Studies Centre, Library & R.O. Barnstaple.
41-91: North Devon: holdings nearly complete for
North Devon.

Cornwall Record Office, Truro.
41-81: parishes at any time in Cornwall (see
Westcountry Studies Library entry above).

South Devon Area Central Library, Torquay.
Abbotskerswell 41,81,91; Ashburton 81,91 (pt);
Ashprington 51-71,91; Awliscombe 41; Berry
Pomeroy 41,61,71,91; Bickington 81,91; Bickleigh
41; Blackborough 41; Bradninch 41; Brixham 41-91;
Shipping 71-91; Broadhembury 41; Broadhempston
41,81,91; Buckerell 41; Buckland in the Moor
41,81,91; Cadbury 41; Cadeleigh 41; Church
Stanton 41; Churston Ferrers 41-81; Clovelly 41;
Cockington 41-91; Coffinswell 41-91; Collumpton
41; Combeinteignhead 81,91; Dartington 71,91;
Dartmouth St. Petrox, St. Saviour. Townstall 51-91;
Shipping 71,91; Denbury 41,81,91; Dittisham
51-71,91; Feniton 41; Haccombe 81,91; Hartland
41; Halberton 41; Lit Hempston 41,71,91; Highweek
81,91; Ilsington 81,91; Ipplepen 41,81,91;
Kentisbeare 41; Kingskerswell 41-91; Kingsteignton
61(pt),81; Kingswear 41-91; Marldon 41-91;
Netherexe 41; Newton Abbot Wolborough
71(pt),81,91; Workhouse 71,91; E and W Ogwell
81,91; Paignton 41-91; Payhembury 41; Plymtree
41; Rewe 41; Sampford Peverell 41; Sheldon 41;
Silverton 41; Staverton 41,91; Stoke Gabriel 41-91;
Stokeinteignhead 51-91; Talaton 41; Teigngrace
61,81,91; Thorverton 41; Torbryan 41,61,81,91;
Torquay St. Marychurch 41-91; Torquay Tormoham
41-91; Shipping 71,91; Totnes 51-71,91; Uplowman
41; Welcombe 41; Widecombe 41,81,91; Willand
41; Wolborough 41-91; Woodland 81,91;
Woolfardisley 41; Yarnscombe 41.
61: Additional parishes on microfilm.

Reference Library, Dorchester, Dorset.
Axminster 51,71-91; Axmouth 51,81; Chardstock
41,51,71-91; Colyton 51,81; Coombpyne 51,71;
Dalwood 41-61,81,91; Hawkchurch 41,51,71,81;
Kilmington 51,71,81,91; Membury 51-91; Musbury
51,61,81; Seaton in Beer 51,61,81; Shute 51,61,81;
Stockland 41-91; Thorncombe 51-91; Uplyme
51-81.

Somerset Record Office, Taunton.
Bampton 51; Burlescombe 61-81; Clayhanger 51;
Clayhidon 51-81; Culmstock 61-81; Hemyock
61-81; Hockworthy 51; Holcombe Rogus 61-81;
Morebath 51,71,81; Yarcombe 51-81.

DORSET

Census Indexes and Publications:
   See *Marriage, Census and Other Indexes* for
Somerset and Dorset FHS published indexes to
whole county 1851 (15 vols.).

Dorset Record Office, Dorchester.
41-91: county of Dorset.

Reference Library, Dorchester, Dorset.
41-91: whole county.

Lansdowne Library, Bournemouth.
51,61,81,91: Canford, Chalbury, Hampreston (also
41), Hinton Martel, Hinton Parva, Kinson, W Parley,
Wimborne (81 pt only), Witchampton.
51,91 only: Corfe Mullen, Edmondsham, Holton,
Longfleet, Parkstone, Poole, Shapwick, Sturminster
Marshall, Woodlands.

Poole Reference Library.
41: Poole, St.James; Blandford; Wimborne.
51: Poole St.James. **61:** Parkstone. **71:** Blandford.
81: Wimborne; Canford Magna; Kinson.
91: Dorset.

Westcountry Studies Library, Exeter.
51-91: Charstock, Charmouth, Hawkchurch, Lyme
Regis; Beerhall Tithing 51-81, Axminster 61-81;
Thorncombe 41-91.

Somerset Record Office, Taunton.
Bradford Abbas 71,81; Broadwinsor 81; Buckhorn
Weston 51,61,81; Cheddington 71; Clifton Maybank
71,81; Nether and Over Compton 71,81; Haydon
71,81; Kington Magna 51,61,81; Mosterton 71;
Oborne 81; Netherbury 81; Nettlecombe 81; S
Perrot 71; Purse Caundle 71,81; Whitchurch 81.

Yeovil Library (Somerset C.C.).
41: hundreds of Corfe Castle; Bere Regis;
Hundredsbarrow; Hasilor; Rowbarrow; Winfrith;
Bindon; Owermoigne Liberty; Beaminster Forum
and Redborne Hundred; Eggerton; Godderthorne;
Whitchurch Canonicorum; Broadwinsor Liberty;
Frampton Liberty; Lothers and Bothenhampton
Liberty; Eggerton; Poorstock Liberty; Culliford Tree;
Buckland Newton; Cerne, Totcombe and Modbury;
Whiteway; Alton Pancras; Piddletrenthide Liberty;
Sydling St. Nicholas Liberty; George; Puddletown
Tollerford; Uggscombe; Fordington Liberty; Sutton
Poyntz Liberty; Isle of Portland Liberty; Piddlehinton
Liberty; Badbury; Cogdean; Cranborne; Knowlton;
Sixpenny Handley; Badbury; Loosebarrow; Monck-
ton-up-Wimborne; Wimborne St.Giles; Gillingham;
Sherborne; Yetminster; Halstock Liberty;

Dorset: *Yeovil Library* continued
Ryme Intrinseca Liberty; Brownshall; Redland;
Sturminster Newton Castle; Stower Provost Liberty;
Blandford Borough; Bridport Borough; Dorchester
Borough; Lyme Regis Borough; Poole Borough;
Shaftesbury Borough; Alcester Liberty; Sherborne
Borough; Wareham Borough; Stoborough Liberty;
Weymouth and Melcombe Regis Borough.
51: Registration Districts of, Sturminster;
Dorchester;Sherborne; Beaminster.
61,71: Registration Districts of; Shaftesbury;
Sturminster; Weymouth; Dorchester; Sherborne;
Beaminster. **71:** Axminster.
81: Shaftesbury; Sturminster; Blandford; Dorches-
ter; Sherborne; Beaminster; Bridport; Axminster.
91: as 81 but excluding Shaftesbury, and Blandford.

Wiltshire Record Office, Trowbridge.
51-91: Bourton, Silton.

Co. DURHAM
Tyneside now in Tyne & Wear; Teesside now in
Cleveland.

Census Indexes and Publications:
 See *Marriage, Census and Other Indexes* for
Cleveland FHS 1851 census published indexes.

Durham County Record Office.
41-91: whole (historic) county.
Index of street names.
See DCRO Handlist **5**, *Census Indexes*, for indexes
(mainly 1851).

Durham County Library.
41-91 (post-1974 county only) divided between
Durham (City) and *Darlington Branch Libraries.*
Darlington, Teesdale and Sedgefield (pt) Union
Districts at *Darlington*, remainder at *Durham.*

Darlington Branch Library (see also above).
Aislaby 41; Archdeacon Newton 41-91; Barforth
41-91; Billingham 41,51,91; Blackwell 51-81; Bolam
41,91; Bowlees 71,81; Bradbury 41,61-91; Bradbury
and Isles 51,71,81; Brierton 41; Gt Burdon
41-61,81,91; Carlbury 41-71; Carlton 41; Claxton
41,51,91; Coatsay Moor 41-71; Cowpen Bewley
51,91; Dalton Piercy 41,91; Egglescliffe 41; Elstob
41,51; Elton 41; Elwick 41,91; Elwick Hall 41; Frith
61-81; Goosepool 41-71,91; Greatham 41,51,91;
Hart 41; Hartburn 41; Hartlepool 41,91; Haverton
Hill 51,91; Houghton-le-Side 41; Hury 61-81; Long
Newton 41; Low Dinsdale 51-81; Newsham 41;
Newton Bewley 51; Norton 41; Oak Tree
41,51,71,91; Preston upon Tees 41,91; Red
Marshall 41; Seaton Carew 41,51,91; Gt Stainton
41,51,91; Stillington 41,51,91; Stockton-on-Tees
41,91; Stranton 41,51; Thorpe 41,61-81; Thorpe
Thewles 41; Throston 41,91; Whitton 41,91;
Wolviston 41,51,91.

Co. Durham continued

Gateshead Central Library.
Barlow 71; Barmston 51-81; Beamish 41,81; S
Biddick 51; Bill Quay 91; Birtley 41-91; Blaydon
51-81; Bleach Green 71; Boldon 41; Broom 41;
Burnmoor 51,81; Byers Green 41; Chester-le-Street
41,51,81; Chopwell 41-71,91; Cocken 51,81;
Coundon Grange 41; Crawcrook 41-71,91;
Crookgate 71; Dunston 41-91; Edmondsley 51,81;
Eighton Banks 91; Fellside 71; Felling 91;
Gateshead 41-91; Gateshead Fell 41,51; Harraton
41-81; Harton 41; Hedworth 41; Heworth 41-91;
Jarrow 41; Kibblesworth 51,81,91; Lambton 51;
Lamesley 41-91; Lintz Green 41; Low Fell 91; Gt
and Lit Lumley 51,81; Marley Hill 51,71-91; Monkton
41; Muggleswick 41; Ouston 41-81; Pelton 41-81;
Plawsworth 41,71,81; Ravensworth 41-71; Ryton
41-91; Ryton Woodside 41-71; South Shields 41;
Stanley 41; Stella 41-71,91; Swalwell 41-91;
Tanfield 41; Urpeth 41,51,71,81; Usworth 51,71,81;
Gt Usworth 51; Waldridge 41,51,81; Washington
51-81; Whickham 41-91; Windy Nook 91; Winlaton
41-91; Witton Gilbert 41,51,71,81.
51: print-out and card index to heads of families.

Tyne & Wear Archives Service, Blandford Square,
Newcastle-upon-Tyne.
41-91: Tyne & Wear.

South Tyneside Central Library (Local History
Dept.), South Shields.
41-91: South Tyneside, comprising South Shields,
Jarrow, Hebburn, The Boldons, Cleadon village and
Whitburn.

Sunderland Central Library.
41: City of Sunderland and towns of Houghton,
Hetton and Washington.
51-71: City of Sunderland only.
81: Sunderland district.
91: City of Sunderland.

Berwick-upon-Tweed Record Office.
41-91: North Northumberland (Berwick-upon-
Tweed, Norham and Islandshire, and Glendale and
Belford Unions).

Cleveland County Libraries, Archives Dept.,
Exchange House, 6 Marton Road, Middlesbrough;
and *Middlesbrough Central Library.*
41-91: those parts of pre-1974 Co. Durham (incl.
Stockton-on-Tees, Hartlepool and Billingham) now
in Cleveland.

Hartlepool Library.
41-91: Hartlepool area (name index by Cleveland
FHS).

Stockton-on-Tees Library.
41-91: District of Stockton-on-Tees.
1851 name index (Cleveland FHS).

Stockton-on-Tees Museum, 76 Norton Road.
41-81: Stockton (also TS transcript of 41.)

ESSEX

Census Indexes and Publications:
See *Marriage, Census and Other Indexes* for Essex SFH 1851 census transcript, microfiche publication; East of London FHS 1851 and 1861 census index booklets; and
A Genealogist's Guide to the Essex Record Office (Essex RO, 3rd ed. 1993).

Essex Record Office, Chelmsford.
41-91: Essex complete.
Index of names, occupations, streets, West Ham 51.
Analysis of households (names other than heads normally omitted): **51,** Chelmsford, Coggeshall, Halstead, Harlow, Markshall, Waltham Holy Cross.
51: Essex SFH microfiche index of names, 11 registration districts (in progress).
61: part of Romford RD.
81: street index to East Ham, West Ham, Little Ilford.
41-81: Panfield name index.
41-91: name index to Burnham and Creeksea.

Essex Record Office, Southend Branch.
51: Bocking, Braintree, Canewdon, Chelmsford, Gt and Lit Coggeshall, Dedham, Harwich, Leigh, Markshall, Rochford, Shalford, Saffron Walden.
71: Leigh.

Essex Record Office, Colchester and N.E. Essex.
51: Analysis sheets from the 51 returns giving full details by households, for the parishes of Harwich and Dovercourt.
51: Essex SFH microfiche for the following districts: Billericay; Great Baddow; Chelmsford: Colchester; Epping: Harwich; Lexden; Maldon; Ongar; Orsett; Rochford; Tendring; Writtle; Great Waltham.

Essex Libraries: Colchester Central Library (Local Studies).
41-91: Essex complete (incl. London Boroughs formerly part of Essex).

Chelmsford Library.
51: Essex.

Southend Central Library (Local Studies).
41: Rochford division.
51-91: former borough of Southend, but also including Ashingdon, Barling, S Benfleet, Canewdon, Canvey Island, Eastwood, S Farnbridge, Foulness Island, Hadleigh, Haveringore Island, Hawkwell, Hockley, Leigh, Paglesham, Prittlewell, Rawreth, Rayleigh, Rochford, N and S Shoebury, Shopland, Southchurch, Southend, Gt Stambridge, Sutton, Thundersley, Gt and Lit Wakering, Wallisea Island.

Grays Central Library.
41: Barstable and Chafford Hundreds.
61: Orsett Union boundaries (corresponding roughly to present Borough of Thurrock).
71-91: As 61 but including various vessels moored in the Thames.

Loughton Library.
Chigwell incl Buckhirst Hill 51 (transcript); Loughton 51-81 (paper copy); Epping incl Epping Upland 71 (paper copy).

Saffron Walden Library.
(the following list is by no means comprehensive, space permits only an abbreviated list).
Arkesden 51-91; Ashdon 51-91; Ashen 51-91; Birdbrook 41-91; Gt and Lit Chesterford 61-81; Chrishall 51,61,81; Clavering 41-91; Debden 41-91; Elmdon 41-91; Hadstock 41-91; Helions Bumpstead 41-91; Hempstead 41-91; Langley 41-91; Littlebury 41-91; Newport 41-91; Radwinter 41-91; Rickling 41-91; Saffron Walden 61-91; Gt Sampford 41-91; Lt Sampford 41-71,91; Steeple Bumpstead 41-91; Strethall 41-91; Wendon Lofts 41,91; Wendons Ambo 41-91; Weston 51,61,81,91; Wicken Bonhunt 41-91; Wickhambrook 51-81; Widdington 41-91; Wimbish 41-91; Gt and Lit Wratting 51-81.
Gt and Lit Abington 51-91; Balsham 51-81; Bartlow 51-91; Castle Camps 51-71; Duxford 51,61,81,91; Hildersham 51-91; Hinxton 51,61,81,91; Horseheath 51,61,81; Ickleton 51,61,81,91; Linton 51-91; Pampisford 51,61,81,91; Sawston 51,61,81,91; Shudy Camps 51-91; Whittlesford 51,61,81,91.

Waltham Abbey Library.
51-81: Waltham Abbey (paper copy).
91: Waltham Abbey on microfilm.

Hertfordshire County Library, Hertford.
Waltham Abbey 51,81.

University of Essex Library, Colchester.
51-71: Braintree (61,71 Bocking area only); Colchester, Halstead districts.

LB of Barking and Dagenham: Valence Reference Library.
Barking and Dagenham 51 (mf enlargements); 41,61-91 (mf).
Indexes, 51 only (appointment necessary).

LB of Havering: Romford Central Library.
41-81: Collier Row, Cranham, Harold Wood, Havering-atte-Bower, Hornchurch, Noak Hill, Rainham, Romford (incl Workhouse), Upminster, Gt Warley.
41 only: Aveley, Brentwood, Childerditch, Grays, Gt and Lit Hallingbury, Harlow, Hatfield Broad Oak, Latton, Matching, Nettleswell, N and S Ockendon, Gt and Lit Parndon, Purfleet, Roydon, Sheering, Stifford, W Thurrock, Llt Warley, S Weald, Wennington.
61: part of Barking.
51-81: part of Dagenham.
91: Stratford, West Ham, East Ham, Leyton, Walthamstow, Chigwell, Chipping Ongar, Romford, Ilford, Barking Town, Hornchurch, Grays, Brentwood, Wickford (piece number order).

Essex continued

LB of Newham: Stratford Reference Library (Local Studies), Water Lane, London E15 4NJ.
East Ham 41-91, and Little Ilford 41-61 (photocopy); 71,81 (mf).
West Ham 41,51 (photocopy); 61-91 (mf).
Indexes: **East Ham** names, occupations 41-61; streets 41-81; **West Ham** names, occupations 41,51; names (pt) 61; streets 51-81.
91: partial index for names for Stratford and Forest Gate using *Kelly's Directory* 1891.

LB of Redbridge: Ilford Central Library.
41: Barking; Gt Ilford and Chadwell wards; Wanstead, Woodford.
51: as above plus Chapel End.
61-81: Barking; Gt Ilford and Chadwell wards; Wanstead; Walthamstow; Woodford.
91: Ilford, Wanstead, Woodford.

LB of Waltham Forest: Vestry House Museum, Vestry Road, Walthamstow, London E17 9NH.
41: Epping, Chingford, Leyton, Nazeing, Roydon, Waltham Holy Cross, Walthamstow (incomplete).
51-71: Chingford, Leyton, Walthamstow (photocopy).
81: Chigwell, Chingford, Leyton, Theydon Bois, Walthamstow, Wanstead, Woodford.
91: Chingford, Leyton, Walthamstow, Woodford.

County Record Office, Cambridge.
41: Ardley; Ashwell; Bygrave; Calecot; Clothall; Cottered; Hinxworth; Kelshall; Radwell; Reed; Royston; Rushdem; Sandon; Therfield; Wallington.
For **61**, except Chrishall, also at *R.O., Huntingdon*: Bartlow Hamlet 51-91; Gt and Lit Chishill 41-91; Chrishall 41; Hadstock 51-91; Heydon 41-91.
Transcript and index: Hadstock 51.

Suffolk Record Office, Bury St. Edmunds.
51-91: Essex parishes bordering on Suffolk.

GLOUCESTERSHIRE and BRISTOL
Southern Gloucestershire and Bristol now in Avon.

Census Indexes and Publications:
 See *Marriage, Census and Other Indexes* for Bristol and Avon FHS 1851 published index and search services, Bristol and Bath districts.
 See also Gloucestershire Record Office, below, 1851 index.

Gloucestershire Record Office.
(A daily charge is made.)
51: whole county (ancient boundaries). Slip index of individuals for the county excluding Bristol available at RO, giving place, place of birth, age.

Gloucestershire and Bristol continued

Gloucester Library.
41-91: complete county, incl Bristol, but *excluding* places in returns for other counties as follows: Admington 41,51,71; Alstone 41; Ashley 41; Aston Subedge 61; Batsford 61,71; Berrington 61-81; Blockley 41,71; Bourton on the Hill 61,71; Chaceley 41; Chipping Camden 51,71; Clopton 41-71; Lit Compton 51,61,81,91; Cutsdean 41; Dorsington 61; Ebrington 711; Evenlode 51; Hunton on the Green 81; Kemble 41; Kingswood (or Wotton-under-Edge) 41; Long Newnton 41; Lower Lemington 71,81; Mangotsfield 61,71; Mickleton 71; Minety 51-91; Moreton in Marsh 71; Oldham 41,61,71; Poole Keynes 41; Poulton 41; Quinton 71; Redmarley 41; Saintbury 61; Shenington 51-91; Somerford Keynes 41; Staunton (Ledbury) 41; Stauntton (W Dean) 41; Sutton under Brailes 61-81; Teddington 41; Todenham 41; Welford on Avon (half of) 41); Weston on Avon 61; Widford 51-91.

Bristol Central Reference Library.
41-91 unless otherwise shown: Abson; Acton Turville; Alderley 51,71-91; Alkington 51,81,91; Almondsbury; Alveston; Aust 41,51,71,91; Gt Badminton 51-91; Berkeley; Bitton; Broadstone 51,61,91; Bulley 41; N Cerney 41; Charfield 51-91; Charlton; Chedworth 41; Chipping Sodbury; Clifton 41-61,81,91; Codrington; Cold Ashton; Compton Greenfield; Cowley 41; Cranham 41; Cromhall 51-91; Cubberley 41; Dodington; Downend; Doynton; Duntisbourne 41; Dyrham; Elberton; Elkstone 41; Filton; Frampton Cotterell; Frenchay; Hallen; Ham 51,71,81; Hambrook; Hamfallow 51-91; Hanham; Hawkesbury 51-91; Henbury; Hill; Hinton (Dyrham); Hinton (Broadstone) 51,61,91 Horfield; Horton 51-91; Huntley 41; Iron Acton; Lit Sodbury; Littleton on Severn; W Littleton; Lr and Upr Longhope 41; Mangotsfield; Marshfield; Minsterworth 41; Nibley 61-71; Northwick 41,61-71,91; Nympsfield 41; Old Land; Old Sodbury; Olveston; Pucklechurch; Rangeworthy 51,71,81; Redwick 41,61-71,91; Rendcombe 41; Rockhampton; Siston; Soundwell; Staple Hill; **41-91:** Stapleton; Stoke Gifford; Stowick 41; Syde 41; Thornbury; Tibberton (pt) 41; Tomarton; Tortworth 51-91; Tytherington; Wapley; Westbury-on-Trym; Westerleigh; Wickwar 51-91; Winterbourne; Yate.

Bristol Record Office, Smeaton Road, Bristol.
81: Census Index (Mormon) for Gloucestershire.
91: Roughly the area covered by the Archdeaconry of Bristol i.e. the area for which they hold parish registers; see also under Somerset section.

Cheltenham Central Libary.
41: Cheltenham incl. Charlton Kings, Leckhampton and Swindon.
51-91: Cheltenham incl. Badgeworth, Charlton Kings, Coberley, Leckhampton, Prestbury, Shurdington, Staverton, Swindon, Uckington, Gt Witcombe.

Gloucestershire continued

Bingham Library, Cirencester.
41-91: Cirencester area.

Tewkesbury Library
41-91: Tewkesbury area.

Cinderford, Stroud and *Stow-on-the-Wold Libraries:*
81 (index), **91**: own areas.

Hereford & Worcester Record Office, Worcester HQ, County Hall, Spetchley Road, Worcester.
41: Alstone, Blockley, Chaceley, Church Iccomb, Cutsdean, Daylesford, Evenlode, Redmarley D'Abitot, Staunton, Teddington, Lit Washbourne.
51 only: Teddington.
51-91: Aston Subedge, Saintbury, Weston Subedge, Willersey.

Centre for Oxon Studies, Oxford Central Library.
91: Complete county.
Lechlade 51-81; Westcote 51,61.

Somerset Record Office, Taunton.
51-81: Bitton, Hanham (71,81 only), Mangotsfield, Oldland, Siston.
81: County transribed index (Mormon)..

Warwickshire Record Office, Warwick.
Batsford 51,61,81,91; Berrington 51, Blockley 51-81; Bourton-on-the-Hill 51-91; Campden, Broad 51; Campden, Chipping 51-91; Clopton 51-91; Combe 51; Ebrington 51-91; Hidcote Bartrim 51,91; Hidcote Boyce 51-91; Lemington, Lower 51-91; Mickleton 51-91; Moreton-in-the-Marsh 51-91; Stoke, Lark 51; Todenham 51-91; Westington 51.

Birmingham Central Library (Local Studies Dept.).
51: Alderminster, Blockley, Chipping Campden, Mickleton, Moreton-in-the-Marsh.

Wiltshire Record Office, Trowbridge.
41: Ashley, Kemble, Kingswood (Wotton-u-Edge), Long Newnton, Pool Keynes, Poulton, Shorncote, Somerford Keynes.

Berkshire Record Office, Reading.
51-91: Lechlade.

HAMPSHIRE and the ISLE OF WIGHT
Bournemouth area now in Dorset; Isle of Wight now a separate county.

Census Indexes and Publications:
  See *Marriage, Census and Other Indexes* for Hampshire 1851 index published by Hampshire GS.
  The Religious Census of Hampshire 1851, ed. J.A. Vickers, Hampshire C.C. **12**, 1993.

Hampshire Record Office, Winchester.
41-91: Hampshire and Isle of Wight.
Transcripts: Denmead Tithing of Hambledon parish 61; New Alresford 61,71; Southampton Holy Rood (indexed) 41.
91: Street index for Portsmouth and Southampton.

Hampshire continued

Isle of Wight Record Office, Newport.
41-91: Isle of Wight complete.

Winchester Library.
81: Hampshire, incl. Bournemouth, Christchurch, Isle of Wight; excl. Portsmouth and Southampton.

Portsmouth Central Library.
41-91: Portsmouth and environs (Gosport, Fareham, Havant and Hayling Island, with places in between, also some up the A3 but not as far as Petersfield).

Southampton Central Library.
41-91 unless stated otherwise. Beaulieu (part of) 41; Botley 41-81; Bursledon 41-81; Chilworth 41-81; Dibden 41; Droxford (Bishops Waltham SD only) 91; Exbury with Lepe 41; Fawley 41; RD Fordingbridge 91; Hamble 41-81; Hound 41-81; RD Lymington 91; Millbrook 41-81; RD New Forest; North Stoneham 41-81; RD Ringwood 91; Romsey 91; South Stoneham; Saint Mary Extra 41-81; Winchester (Twyford and Hursley SD only).

Lansdowne Reference Library, Bournemouth.
Breamore 41,51,91; Burley 41,51,91; N Charford 41; Christchurch 41-91; Damerham 51; Fllingham 41-51,91; Fordingbridge 41,51,91; Foulford 41; Godshill 41,91; Hale 41,51,91; Harbridge 41,51,91; Holdenhurst 41-91; Ibsley 41,51,91; Linford 41; Linwood 41; Martin 51,91; Ogdens 41; Picket Post and Picket Postgate 41; Ringwood 41,51,91; Rockbourne 41,51,91; Shobley 41; Sopley 41-91; Tidpit 51,91; Whitsbury 51,91; Woodgreen 41,91.

Poole (Dorset) Reference Library.
91: Christchurch, Bournemouth, Ringwood.

Wiltshire Record Office, Trowbridge.
Abbots Ann 51; Amport 51-71; Andover 51; Appleshaw 51; Barton Stacey 51; Bramshaw 41; Breamore 51; Bullington 51; Charford 51; Chilbolton 51; Upr Clatford 51; Coombe 51,61,81; Damerham 41,51; Faccombe 51-71; Fordingbridge (pt) 51; Foxcott 51; Fyfield 51-71; Goodworth Clatford 51; Grately 51-71; Hale 51; Hurstbourne Tarrant 51-71; Kimpton 51-71; Knights Enham 51; Linkenholt 51-71; Longparish 51; Martin 41,51; Melchet Park 41,51; Monxton 51-71; New Forest EPPs 51; Penton Mewsey 51; Plaitford 41; Quarley 51-71; Rockbourne 51; Shipton Bellinger 51-71; Tangley 51-71; Thruxton 51-71; S Tidworth 51-71; Vernhams Dean 51-71; W Wellow 41; Wherwell 51; Whitsbury 41,51.

Surrey Record Office, Woking (from mid-1998).
Aldershot 51,61; Bramshott 51; Farnborough 51,61; Hawley 51; Headley 51; Kingsley 51; Long Sutton 51,61; Yateley 51,61.

Berkshire Record Office, Reading
Combe 51-91; Mortimer West End 71.

HEREFORDSHIRE

Now part of Hereford & Worcester.

Hereford City Library.
41-91: complete county (excl. **51:** Radnorshire RDs: Brilley, Eardisley, Huntington, Willersley, Winforton; **71,81:** Newent RD: Aston Ingham, Linton; Knighton RD: Brampton Bryan, Bucknell, Leintwardine (Adforton, Stanway, Paytoe and Grange; Walford, Letton and Newton); Hay RD: Bredwardine, Clifford, Cusop, Dorstone, Whitney; Tenbury RD: Brimfield, Lit Hereford, Stoke Bliss; Monmouth RD: Ganarew, Ganway, Llanrothall, Welsh Bickner, Welsh Newton, Whitchurch;
71: Presteigne RD: Byton, Upr Kinsham, Knill, Lingen, Presteigne (Lit Brampton, Combe, Lr Kinsham, Nash, Rodd, Stapleton, Willey); Ludlow RD: Ludford, Richards Castle;
81: Ludlow RD: Aston, Burrington, Dounton, Elton, Leinhall Starkes, Ludford, Richards Castle, Wigmore.

Hereford & Worcester Record Office, Hereford Branch.
41-91: complete county (excl. Hay area 41-81, Monmouth area 61-81; Leintwardine area 81). 81: Index to Herefordshire.

Powys County Library HQ, Llandrindod Wells.
Adforton 51-81; Barton 61; Bradnor 51,61; Brampton Brian 51-91; Bredwardine 51-91; Brilley 51,61; Buckton 61,71,91; Byton 51-71; Chickward 51,61; Clifford 51-91; Combe 51-71; Coxhall 71; Cusop 51,71,81,91; Dorstone 51-91; Eardisley 51,61,91; Hardwick 81; Hergest 51,61; Huntingdon 51,61,91; Kington 51,61; Old Kington 51; Kinsham 51-71; Knill 51-71; Letton 51-91; Lilwall 51,61; Leintwardine 51,61,81; Lingen 51-71; Lyonshall 51,61; Nash 51-71; Newton 91; Pember Oak 51,61; Pembridge 51,61; Rodd 51-71; Rushock 51,61; Stapleton 51,71; Staunton on Arrow 51,91; Stowe 51-91; Titley 51,61; Walford 51-91; Weston 61; Whitney 51-91; Willey 51,71; Willersley 51; Winforton 51,61,91.

Hereford & Worcester Record Office, Worcester HQ.
41 only: Acton Beauchamp, Edvin Loach, Mathon. **51-91:** Brimfield, Little Hereford.

Shropshire Records, Shrewsbury.
41-91: Herefordshire places near Ludlow.

HERTFORDSHIRE

Publication
  Religion in Hertfordshire 1847 to 1851, ed. Judith Burg, Herts. R.S., 1995 (survey by William Upton for Herts. Union and 1851 Religious Census).

Hertfordshire Local Studies Library, Hertford.
41-91: complete county.

St. Albans Library.
41-81: St. Albans district (41 incomplete).

Welwyn Garden City Central Library.
41-91: Ayot St. Lawrence; Ayot St. Peter; Lemsford (not 41); Tewin; Welwyn; Welwyn Garden City (site of).

Hemel Hempstead Library.
41-91: Hemel Hempstead; most of Dacorum area, incl. Tring, Berkhamsted, Flamsted, Kings Langley. Personal name index (arranged by surname), 51.

Stevenage Central Library.
41-91: Stevenage and area.

LB of Barnet Local History Library, Ravensfield House, The Burroughs, Hendon NW4 4BE.
41-81: present LB of Barnet: Chipping and East Barnet, Totteridge.

Ashwell Field Studies Centre, Merchant Taylors School, Ashwell, Baldock. SG7 5LY.
Ashwell 41-91; Bishops Stortford (pt) 51; Datchworth 51-81; Digswell 51,71; Harpenden 61,71; Kelshall 51,61; Letchworth 51,61,71; North Mymms 51,61; Rushden 51; Sandon 51; Stevenage 51; Therfield 51; Wallington 51; Wheathampstead 61.

Bedfordshire Record Office, Bedford.
61: Ickleford, Ippolitts, Kimpton, Kings Walden. **71:** Codicote, Hexton, Hitchin. **81:** Hitchin, Ickleford, Ippolitts, Kimpton, Kingswalden. **91:** Hitchin, Langley and Preston, Ickleford, St. Ippolitts, Kimpton, Kings Walden, Lilley, Offley, St. Pauls's Walden, Pirton.

Buckinghamshire County Library, Aylesbury and Milton Keynes, High Wycombe.
41-91: some parishes in Berkhampstead and Tring areas bordering Buckinghamshire.
41-81: parishes bordering on Bucks.

Cambridgeshire Record Office, Cambridge.
41,61-91: Ashwell, Hinxworth, Kelshall, Reed, Royston, Therfield.
41: Ardley, Bradfield, Bygrave, Caldecot, Clothall, Cottered, radwell, Rushden, Sandon, Wallington.
61-91: Barkway, Barley.
81: Mormon fiche index to county.

Cambridgeshire Record Office, Huntingdon.
61,71: Ashwell, Barkway, Barley, Hinxworth, Kelshall, Reed, Royston (Herts. portion), Therfield.
81: Transcript (Mormon).

HUNTINGDONSHIRE
Now part of Cambridgeshire.

See *Genealogical Sources in Cambridgeshire,
Cambs RO*, second edition 1994, for exact location
of 41-91 census mf for all parishes.

Census Index:
Huntingdonshire 1851: Whole county
transcribed, indexed transcripts at *Cambridge* and
Huntingdon Record Offices and *Society of
Genealogists.* See *Marriage, Census and Other
Indexes* for microfiche copies and search service.

*County Record Office (Cambridgeshire C.C.),
Huntingdon.*
41-81: complete county.
Transcripts and indexes for most parishes.
41:'Censearch' surname index, indexed transcripts.
51: for all **county.**
61-71: transcripts for parishes Giddings,
Hammerton district.
81: surname index for Caxton, Huntingdon, St. Ives,
St. Neots districts (Hunts FHS) and Mormon index.
91: Ramsey, Somersham and Warboys SDs.

Cambridgeshie Record Office, Cambridge.
Abbotsley 61,91; Lt. Barford 91; Buckdon 91;
Diddington 61,91; Eynesbury 71,91; Farcet 51;
Fletton 61,71; Grafham 61,91; Gt Gransden 51-91;
Offord Cluny and Darcy 61,91; Orton Longueville
(pt) 51; Papworth St Agnes 51-91; Gt and Lit Paxton
61,91; St. Neots 71,91; Southoe 61,91; Stanground
51-71; Tetworth 61-91; Toseland 61-91; Waresley
61,91; Woodston 61,71; Yelling 61-91.
51: Transcripts and indexes for whole county.
81: Whole county and Mormon fiche indexes.
91: Ramsey, Gt and Lt Raveley, Upwood (trans).

Peterborough Library (Cambs. C.C.).
Transcript and index **51:** Stilton Sub-district
(Alwalton; Caldecote; Chesterton; Denton; Farcet;
Folksworth; Glatton; Haddon; Holme; Morborne;
Orton Longueville and Waterville, Stilton,
Washingley and Yaxley).
41-91: Alwalton; Caldecote; Chesterton; Denton;
Farcet; Fletton; Folksworth; Glatton; Haddon;
Holme; Morborne; Orton Longueville and Waterville;
Stanground; Stilton; Washingley; Water Newton;
Woodston; Yaxley. Stamford RD: Stibbington and
Sibson.
(Oundle RD): **41,61,71,81:** Elton **51:** Gt. and Lt
Gidding, Thurning, Winwick.

Bedfordshire Record Office, Bedford.
Abbotsley 61, 81,91; Catworth 61-91; Diddington
61,81,91; Graveley 61-91; Hail Weston 71-91 ;
Kimbolton 61-91; Offord D'Arcy and Cluny,
61,81,91; Gt and Lit Paxton 61,81,91; Southoe,
61,81,91; Gt Staughton 61-91; Stow Longa 61-91;
Tetworth 51-91; Toseland 61-91; Waresley
61,81,91

Northamptonshire Record Office, Northampton.
51,81 (also 71 where shown): Alwalton; Brington 71;
Bythorn 71; Caldecote; Chesterton; Covington 71;
Denton; Elton 71; Farcet; Fletton 71; Folksworth; Gt
Gidding 71; Lit Gidding; Glatton; Haddon; Holme;
Keystone 71; Luddington 71; Lutton 81 only;
Molesworth 71; Morborne; Old Weston 71; Orton
Longueville and Waterville; Stanground 71;
Stibbington; Stilton; Thurning 71; Washingley;
Water Newton; Winwick 71; Woodstone 71; Yaxley.

KENT

Census Indexes and Publications:
See *Marriage, Census and Other Indexes* for
various index projects and publications.
See also Kent FHS microfiche catalogues for
census indexes, details from R.J. Bailey,
Delft Lodge, Bower Road, Mersham, Ashford,
Kent TN25 6NW.

*Institute of Heraldic and Genealogical Studies,
Northgate, Canterbury CT1 1BA.*
51: All of Kent east of and including Maidstone.

Kent County Library:
Centre for Kentish Studies, Maidstone.
41-91: Complete county.

The following libraries within Kent County Library
have census returns for their own areas, often
varying from census to census.

Ashford Library.
41-91: Ashford Borough or District Council area,
incl. Charing, Chilham, Tenterden, Wye.

Broadstairs Library.
41-91: Broadstairs, St. Peter's (51 also Ramsgate
parishes).

Canterbury Library.
41: Ramsgate and Margate area.
41-51: Chilham, Deal and Wye.
41-91: Canterbury (all parishes); Adisham, Barham,
Bekesbourne, Bishopsbourne, Blean, Bridge,
Chartham, Chislet, Fordwich, Hackington,
Harbledon, Upr and Lr Hardres, Herne, Hoath,
Ickham, Kingston, Littlebourne, Milton, Nackington,
Patrixbourne, Petham. Preston next Wingham,
Stodmarsh, Stourmouth and Wingham, Thanington,
Waltham, Wickhambreaux, Womenswould.
51-91: Reculver, Seasalter, Sturry, Swalecliffe,
Westbere, Whitstable (*Note.* 41 returns do not
survive).

Deal Library.
41-91: Deal and surrounding parishes.

Dover Library.
41-91: Dover District Council area, incl. Dover,
Deal, Sandwich, Ash, Wingham, Eastry.

Kent continued

Dartford Library.
41-91: Ash, Crockenhill (not 41), Darenth, Dartford, Eynesford, Farningham, Fawkham, Greenhithe, Hartley, Hextable, Horton Kirby, Kingsdown, Longfield, Lullingstone, Ridley, Southfleet, Stone, Sutton-at-Hone, Swanley, Swanscombe, Wilmington.
41: Bromley, Beckenham.
41,51: Dartford area, incl. Bexley.

Folkestone Library.
41,61,71: Folkestone, Hawkinge, Cheriton, Sandgate, Hythe (photostat); Romney Marsh area, Elham (mf).
51 (ph'stat), 81 (mf): Shepway District Council area. Index: Hythe 51.
81-91: Shepway DC area and Capel-le-Ferne.

Gillingham Library.
41-81: Chalk, Cobham, Denton, Gravesend, Higham, Luddesdown, Meopham, Milton, Northfleet, Shorne.
41-61: Cliffe, Cuxton, Frindsbury, Halling, Strood.
41,51: Cooling, Ifield, Nurstead.
61,81: Rosherville.
91: Brompton (New), Brompton (Old), Capston, Chatham, Gadshill, Gillingham, Halstow (Lower), Iwade, Lidsing, Luton, Milton next Sittingbourne, Murston, Newington, Rainham, Rodmersham, Sittingbourne, Tong, Tunstall, Upchurch.

Gravesend Library.
Chalk 41-91; Cliffe 41-61; Cobham 41-91; Cooling 41,51; Cuxton 41-61; Denton 41-91; Frindsbury 41-61; Gravesend 41-91; Halling 41-61; Higham 41-91; Ifield 41-91; Luddesdown 41-91; Meopham 41-91; Milton 41-91; Northfleet 41-91; Nurstead 41-91; Rosherville (Northfleet) 61-91; Shorne 41-91; Strood 41-61.

Margate Library.
41-91: Acol (or Wood), Birchington, Broadstairs, Margate, Minster, Monkton, Ramsgate, St. John's, St. Lawrence's, St. Peter's, St. Nicholas, Sarre.
41 only: a much wider area.

Ramsgate Library.
51,61: Broadstairs, Ramsgate, St. Peter's.
71,81: as at Margate Library.

Rochester upon Medway Studies Centre.
41-91: Chatham; Rochester; Isle of Grain; Wouldham.
81-91: Gillingham.
Indexes: 41-81: for Chatham and Rochester; Isle of Grain and Wouldham; 91: Strood and Isle of Grain; 91: Chatham and Rochester in progress.

Sevenoaks Library.
41-91: Sevenoaks area, incl. Edenbridge, Westerham.
Index: 51: Sevenoaks district.

Sheerness Library.
41-91: Isle of Sheppey (all parishes).

Sittingbourne Library.
41-91: Sittingbourne and Faversham areas and Isle of Sheppey.

Tonbridge Library.
41-91: Addington, Aylesford, Birling, Burham, Ditton, Ightham, Leybourne, E and W Malling, Mereworth, Offham, W Peckham, Ryarsh, Snodland and Paddlesworth, Stansted, Tonbridge (41-71 electrostatic prints), Trottiscliffe, Wateringbury, Wouldham, Wrotham.
  Also (electrostatic prints): Brenchley (pt) 51,61; Chiddingstone 51; E Peckham 41-71; Hadlow 41-71; Hildenborough 41-71; Paddock Wood 51; Shipbourne 41-71; Southborough 41-71; Tonbridge 81; Yalding 51.
41 only: a much wider area.
Indexes: 41: Tonbridge (in progress);
51: Tonbridge, Hadlow, Hildenborough, Shipbourne, Southborough;
61: Tonbridge.

Tunbridge Wells Library.
Tunbridge Wells 41-81 (51 in photostat); Ashurst 61-91; Bells Yew Green 61; Bidborough 61-91; Eridge 61; Frant 41,61,91; Groombridge 41,91; Hildenborough 41,61,91; Langton Green 41,61-91; Rusthall 41-81; Southborough 41,61-91; Speldhurst 41,61-91; Teston 41; Thornham 41; Tonbridge 41,61,91(part); Trottiscliffe 41; Tudeley 41,91.

Bexley Local Studies Centre, Hall Place, Bourne Road, Bexley.
41-81: Bexley, Footscray, North Cray, Erith, Crayford and East Wickham.
Indexes: Erith 41; E Wickham 41-61; Bexley 51,81.

Bromley Central Library.
41-81: Beckenham, Bromley, Chelsfield, Chislehurst, Footscray, N Cray, St. Mary Cray, (St.) Pauls Cray, Cudham, Downe, Eltham (incl. Mottingham except 61), Farnborough, Hayes, Keston, Knockholt, Orpington (not 41), West Wickham.
41 only: Ash, Bexley, Brasted, Charlton (also 51), Chevening, Chiddingstone, Cowden, Crayford, Darenth, Dartford, Edenbridge, Erith, Eynsford, Farningham, Fawkham, Halstead, Hartley, Haver, Horton Kirby, Kemsing, Kidbrooke, Kingsdown, Plumstead (51 only), Seal, Sevenoaks (incl. Rivermead and Weald), Shoreham, Southfleet, Stone, Sundridge, Sutton-at-Hone, Swanscombe, Westerham, E Wickham (nr Bexley), Wilmington.
Photocopies: Bromley 51; Orpington 41,51.
Transcripts: Hayes 1821; Farnborough 41; Keston 41-61.

Christ Church College, Canterbury.
51,81: Canterbury, Milton, Faversham, and Thanet RDs.

East Sussex Record Office, Lewes.
41-91: Kent parts of Broomhill, Frant (Broadwater Down) and Lamberhurst.

Kent continued

University of Kent at Canterbury Library.
41,51: Canterbury, Dover, Elham, Hythe (West Hythe 41 only).
41 only: Leaveland, Leysdown, Linstead, Luddenham, Marden, Mersham, Milstead, Milton-next-Sittingbourne, Minster-in-Sheppey, Mol(d)ash, Murston.
51: Sheppey district.
61,71: Milstead sub-district.

LANCASHIRE

Now split between the counties of Lancashire, Greater Manchester and Merseyside; Furness now in Cumbria and southern border area in Cheshire.

Census Indexes and Publications:
   See *Marriage, Census and Other Indexes* for the many index projects and publications available.

   In an attempt to simplify the very complicated holdings, the historic county is divided into its post-1974 component counties, from north to south.

CUMBRIA (Furness and Cartmel area)

Barrow-in-Furness Library.
41-91: whole Furness and Cartmel area.

University of Lancaster.
41-91: Furness and Cartmel area.

Lancaster Library.
41: Furness area as at that date, incl. Coniston, Dalton. Hawkshead, Ulverston, etc.

Cumbria Record Office, Barrow branch.
Transcripts: 41: Penny Bridge; Spark Bridge;
51: Dunnerdale and Seathwaite; Pennington; Ulverston Workhouse.

Cumbria Record Office, Kendal branch.
51: Claife
81: Egton-cum-Newland; Lowick; Ulverston; Hawkshead.
Transcripts: 41: Cartmel Fell.
41,51: Staveley-in-Cartmel and part of Cartmel Fell.
51: Part of Upper Allithwaite and Lindale; Upper Allithwaite and Cartmel Fell; Staveley-in-Cartmel; East Broughton, Grange; part Upper Holker.
51,81: part Lower Allithwaite and Allithwaite.

Lancashire continued

LANCASHIRE (post-1974)

University of Lancaster.
41-91: complete county north of River Ribble.
51: area south of Preston, incl. Walton, Cuerdale.

The Lancashire Library.
41-91 for the whole post-1974 administrative county of **Lancashire**. Normally held in District HQ Library in the area to which they relate, 41-91, but occasional exceptions, so users are advised to contact library concerned prior to making a visit.

Central Library Hyndburn District, Accrington
41-91: Accrington; Altham; Church; Clayton-le-Moors; Gt Harwood, Higham with West Close Booth, Huncoat, Oswaldtwistle; Rishton.
91: Billington; Dinckley; Hapton; Heyhouses; Little Harwood; Padiham; Read; Salesbury; Simonstone; Wilpshire.
Indexes, 51: Altham, Huncoat, Oswaldtwistle.

Barnoldswick Library.
41-91: Admergill (not 51,61); Barnoldswick; Bracewell; Brogden; Coates; Earby (not 41 and 51); Marton's Both; Salterforth; Thornton in Craven.

Blackburn District Central Library.
41-91: Complete for their area.

Blackpool Library.
41-91: Barnacre, Bilsborrow, Bispham with Norbreck, Blackpool, Bleasdale, Bonds, Bryning with Kellamergh, Cabus, Carleton, Catterall, Claughton (nr Garstang), Cleveley (nr Forton), Clifton with Salwick, Gt Eccleston, Lit Eccleston with Larbreck, Elswick, Fleetwood, Forton, Freckleton, Garstang, Greenhalgh with Thistleton, Hambleton, Hardhorn with Newton, Holleth, Inskip with Sowerby, Kirkham, Kirkland, Layton with Warbreck, Lytham, Marton (Blackpool), Medlar with Wesham, Myers-cough, Nateby, Newton with Scales, Pilling, Poulton-le-Fylde, Preesall with Hackensall, Rawcliffe, Ribby with Wrea, Singleton, Stalmine with Staynall, Thorn-ton (nr Blackpool), Treales, Roseacre and Wharles, Warton (nr Kirkham), Weeton with Preese, Westby with Plumpton, Winmarleigh, Nether Wyresdale.

Burnley Library.
41-91: Burnley, Cliviger, Filly Close and New Laund Booth, Habergham Eaves, Hapton, Heyhouses, Huncoat, Ightenhill Park, Padiham, Reedley Hallows, Simonstone, Worsthorne with Hurstwood.
Indexes, 41-81: Heads of households.
91: Street index on cards and head of household.

Chorley Library.
41-91: Adlington; Anglezarke; Bretherton; Brindle; Charnock Richard; Coppull; Croston; Cuerden; Eccleston (nr Chorley); Euxton; Heapey; Heath Charnock; Heskin; Hoghton; Leyland; Mawdesley; Rivington; Shevington; Standish with Langtree; Ulnes Walton; Welch Whittle; Wheelton; Whittle-le-Woods; Withnell; Worthington.

Lancashire (post-1974) continued

Clitheroe Library.
41-81: Aughton, Bowland Forest, Bradford West, Chipping, Clitheroe, Downham, Gisburn, Grindleton, Mearley, Mitton, Paythorne, Pendleton nr Whalley, Ribchester, Rimington, Twiston, Waddington, Whalley, Wiswell.
91: Alston, Balderstone, Barrow, Bashall Eaves, Billington, Bolton by Bowland, Bowland Forest (Higher Div.), Chaigley, Chatburn, Chipping, Clayton le Dale, Clitheroe, Dilworth, Dinckley, Downham, Dutton, Easington, Gisburn, Gisburn Forest, Goldshaw Booth, Grindleton, Heyhouses, Horton, Hurst Green, Knowle Green, Langho, Little Bowland, Leagram, Mearly, Mellor, Middop, Mitton, Newsholme, Newton, Osbaldeston, Paythorne, Pendleton, Ramsgreave, Read, Ribchester, Rimington, Sabden, Salesbury, Sawley, Simonstone, Slaidburn, Stoneyhurst College, Thornley with Wheatley, Tosside, Twiston, Waddington, West Bradford, Whalley, Wilpshire, Wiswell, Worston.

Darwen Library
41-91: Over Darwen; Eccleshill; Yate; Pickup Bank.

Haslingden Library.
41-91: Bury: Cowpe and Lenches; Grane; Newhallhey and Hall Carr; Musbury; Haslingden.
Also Waterfoot: Newhallhey, Cowpe and Lenches 51-91; Bury: Henheads 41-71; Higher Booths 51,61, 91; Goodshaw: Higher Booths 61,71,91; Lumb: Higher Booths 61-81; Lower Booths 51,91; Rawten-stall: Lower Booths 61-81,91; Tottington Higher End 51-91; Edenfield: Tottington Higher End 51-91; Chatterton, Strongsty, Stubbins Vale: Tottington Higher End 71,81; New and Old Accrington, 51.
See also *Rawtenstall Library*; and under Greater Manchester.

Lancaster Library.
41-91: Arkholme with Cawood, Ashton with Stodday, Aughton (Halton), Bare, Borwick, Bulk, Burrow with Burrow (51-91 only), Cantsfield, Carnforth, Caton, Claughton (Lune Valley), Cockerham, Ellel, Farleton, Gressingham, Halton, Heaton with Oxcliffe, Heysham, Hornby, Ireby, Kellet, Lancaster, Leck, Melling with Wrayton, Middleton (nr Lancaster), Overton, Poulton-le-Sands (Morecambe), Priest Hutton, Quernmore, Roeburndale, Scotforth, Silverdale, Skerton, Tatham, Thurnham, Warton with Lindeth, Wennington, Whittington, Wray with Botton, Over Wyresdale, Yealand Conyers and Redmayne.
91: Bentham, Ingleton, Clapham, Burton in Lonsdale, Thornton in Lonsdale.

Leyland Library.
41-91: Cuerdale, Farington, Hoole (Little and Much), Howick, Hutton, Longton, Penwortham, Samlesbury, Walton-le-Dale.
Surname Index 51: Farington, Hoole, Howick, Hutton, Longton, Penwortham.

Nelson Library and Colne Library.
The holdings for the Pendle District are divided between these two libraries, most held by *Nelson*.
41-91: Barley with Wheatley Booth, Barrowford Booth, Barnoldswick (not 81), Bracewell (not 41 or 81), Briercliffe with Extwistle, Brogden (not 41 or 81), Cliviger (part of 91 only), Coates (not 71 or 81), Colne, Earby, Filly Close and New Laund Booth, Foulridge, Goldshaw Booth (not 81), Heyhouses, Higham with West Close Booth, Gt and Lit Marsden (incl. Nelson and Brierfield), Martons Booth (51,71,91), Old Laund Booth, Reedley Hallows, Roughlee Booth, Salterforth, Thornton in Craven, (51,71,91 only), Trawden, Wheatley Carr, Worsthorne with Hurstwood.

Ormskirk Library.
41: Aigburth, Allerton, Childwall, Garston, Hale, Haleswood, Parbold (91 also), Speke, Woolton (Little), Woolton (Much), Wrightington.
51-61: Ainsdale, Banks, Blowick (51 only), Churchtown, Crossens, Marshside, North Meols, Ravenmeols, Southport, Wavertree (51 only).
51-81: Birkdale, **81-91:** Billinge, Dalton, Formby (51,61,71,91); **41-91:** Altcar, Aughton, Bickerstaffe, Bispham, Burscough, Downholland, Halsall, Hesketh-with-Becc, Lathom, Lydiate, Maghull, Melling, Newburgh (41-81 only), Ormskirk, Rufford, Scarisbrick, Simonswood (51-91 only), Skelmersdale, Tarleton; **81:** Upholland; **91:** Shevington, Standish, Worthington.

Preston (Harris) Library.
41-91: Ashton, Barton, Broughton, Cottam, Goosnargh, Grimsargh, Haighton, Ingol, Lea, Preston, Ribbleton, Whittingham, Woodplumpton.

Rawtenstall Library.
41-91: Accrington (New and Old) (41 only), Bacup, Higher and Lower Booths, Brandwood, Catley Lane (61,71 only), Chadwick, Chatterton (51,81 only), Cloughfold, Cowpe with Lench, Crawshawbooth, Edenfield (51,81 only), Facit, Falinge, Goodshaw, Haslingden (81 only), Healey, Littleborough (51 only), Loveclough, Lumb in Rossendale, Musbury (81 only), Newchurch in Rossendale, Newhall Hey and Hall Carr, Rawtenstall, Reedsholme, Spotland, Stacksteads, Stubbins Vale (51,81 only), Strongsty (51,81 only), Tottington Higher End (51,81 only), Waterfoot, Whitworth, Wolstenholme.
91: Ainsworth, Bamford, Burnley, Bury, Darwen, Heap Bridge, Heywood, Milnrow, Radcliffe, Ramsbottom, Summerseat, Todmorden, Tottington Lower End, Walmersley cum Shuttleworth.
See also *Haslingden Library*; and under Greater Manchester

H.Q. Library, Preston.
51: Religious census (pre-1974 county).
Prior appointment essential.

Lancashire Record Office, Preston.
41-61: Whole of **Lancashire** (pre-1974).

Lancashire (post-1974) continued

St. Annes District Central Library.
41-91: Lytham, Great and Little Marton (Blackpool).
51-91: Bryning with Kellamergh, Greenalgh with Thistleton, Medlar with Wesham, Ribby with Wrea, Treales, Roseacre and Wharles, Warton, Weeton with Preese, Westby with Plumpton.
41-81: Great and Little Carleton.
51-81: Elswick, Layton with Warbreck, Little Eccleston with Larbreck.
Also Preston 41, Clifton with Salwick 51,81,91, Kirkham 51,81,91, Freckleton 51,81,91, St.Annes on the Sea 91.

Note. Many of these libraries may also hold duplicates for one or more census years for which other libraries are shown as having the main holdings. For simplicity these incomplete holdings are not normally listed. The *Lancashire University (Poulton Campus, Preston)* also has returns for **51** and **71** for many places in the Preston area, but these should be accessible in the public libraries.

The following libraries outside the present Lancashire have small holdings:

Bolton Reference Library.
(Asterisked returns may be incomplete.)
Adlington 51-91*; Anderton 51-91*; Anglezarke 41-91; Edgworth 41-91; Entwistle 41-91; Haigh 51-71*; Heath Charnock 51-91*; Longworth 41-91; Quarlton 41-91; Rivington 41-91; Sharples 41-91; Turton 41-91; Wheelton 51*; Withnell 51*; Whittle-le-Woods 51*; Wrightington 51.
See *Tracing Your Ancestors in Bolton.*

Knowsley Central Library, Huyton.
91: Aughton; Bispham; Burscough; Hesketh; Lathom; Ormskirk; Rufford; Scarisbrick; Skelmersdale; Tarleton.

St. Helens Local History and Archives Library. Gamble Institute.
41-91: All the modern borough of St. Helens incl. Billinge; Bold; Eccleston; Haydock; Newton-le-Willows; Parr; Rainford; Rainhill; Sutton;

Southport Library.
Great Altcar 41-71; Aughton 41; Banks 41-91; Halsall 81-91; Scarisbrick 91.

Wigan Archives, Town Hall, Leigh (asterisked places also at *Wigan Heritage Services History Shop*).
41 only unless shown otherwise: Anglezark*; Bispham (61 only*); Clayton-le-Woods*; Clitheroe; Cliviger; Colne; Cuerden*; Dalton 41-91; Eccleston* (nr Chorley); Edgeworth*; Entwistle*; Euxton*; Farrington; Gt and Lit Harwood*; Heapy*; Hesketh with Becconsall*; Heath Charnock*; Heskin*; Hoghton; Lathom; Leyland*; Longton; Longworth*; Loveclough; Ormskirk 61; Penwortham; Parbold **41-91:** Quarlton*; Rivington*; Sharples*; Skelmersdale 61 only; Up-holland 41-91*; Wheelton*; Whittle-le-Woods*; Withnall; Wrightington 41-91.

Wigan Heritage Services History Shop (Wigan Reference Library) (see also left).
41: Adlington, Anderton, Charnock Richard, Coppull, Duxbury, Heath Charnock, Howick, Hutton, Hoole (Little and Much), Rufford.

The following key is to 25 libraries & R.O. in Greater Manchester, Merseyside, Cheshire and Lancashire which have holdings outside post-1974 Lancashire.

A	: Blackburn	NN	: Oldham
B	: Bolton	O	: Ormskirk
C	: Bootle	P	: Rawtenstall
D	: Bury	Q	: Rochdale
E	: Chorley	R	: St. Helens
F	: Crosby	S	: Salford
H	: Heywood	T	: Southport
J	: Knowsley	U	: Stalybridge
K	: Leigh Archives	W	: Warrington
KK	: Liverpool R.O.	X	: Widnes
L	: Liverpool	Y	: Wigan Heritage
M	: Manchester		History Shop
N	: Middleton	Z	: Wigan Archives

Note. A hazard of the following lists is that different libraries provide information in differing detail, so smaller places, perhaps part of a town, listed by one library, may be covered by another's listing just of that town. Some places still in Lancashire may be included below, and places now in Greater Manchester and Merseyside appear under Lancashire County libraries. Amendments will be welcome. *Eds.*

4 = 41; 5 = 51; 6 = 61; 7 = 71; 8 = 81; 9=91.
* = possibly incomplete.

GREATER MANCHESTER (post-1974 county)

Abram YZ4-9,R4; Affetside D4-9; Ainsworth B4-5*, D4-9,P4-9; Alkrington D4(pt),N5-9; Ashton-in-Makerfield K9,YZ4-9,R458; Ashton-under-Lyne U4-9; Ashworth D4-9,H589; Aspull YZ4-9,R4,B5-9*; Astley KYZ4-9,W8; Atherton KYZ4-9; Audenshaw U4-9,M78; Baldingstone D4-9; Bamford D4-9,P4-9; Barton C4-8,M567,S4-9; Bedford (Leigh) KYZ4-9, W678; Besses o'th' Barn D4-9; Billinge Chapel End and Higher End YZ4-9; Birch D4-9, H9; Birtle D4-9, H4589; Blackrod A4,B4-9,YZ4-9; Blatchinworth P5,Q4; Blatchinworth and Calderbrook Q5-9; Gt Bolton B4-9; Lit Bolton (nr Bolton) B4-9,A5; Boothstown S4-9; Bradshaw B4-9,A45,YZ4; Brindle Heath S4; Breightmet B4-9,A45,YZ4; Bromyhurst C4; Brooksbottom D4-9; Broughton S4-9,M4-7; Burrs D4-9; Bury D4-9,B4,8*,P4-9; Butterworth Q4; Butterworth (Freeholdside) Q5-9; Butterworth (Lordshipside) Q5679; Cadishead S4-9,M567; Calderbrook P5,Q4; Castleton (without the Borough) Q5-7; Castleton (within the Borough) Q5-7; Castleton (Furtherside) Q89; Castleton (Nearer) Q89; Catley Lane P67; Chadderton NN4-9,D4, N8pt,9pt); Chapelfield D4-9; Chatterton D4-9; Clifton S4-9; Cockey Moor D4-9; Crimble D4-9,H9; Croft K4-6,YZ4-9,S4-8,W5-8; Crompton NN4-9,D4;

Lancashire (Greater Manchester) continued

Cuerdley YZ5; Culcheth R4,KYZ5-9,YZ4,W678; Darcy Lever B4-9,A4,YZ4; Davyhulme S458,M567; Dean YZ5; Delph (Saddleworth) Q56; Denton U4-9, M457; Droylsden U4-9,M4-8; Dumplington S458; Eccles S4-9,M57; Edenfield D4-9; Ellenbrook S4-9; Elton D4-9,B4; Failsworth M4-8,NN4-9; Fairfield M4-8; Falinge P4-8; Fall Bank D4-9; Farnworth B4-9,YZ4,R7,J78; Flixton S5-8,M57; Freetown D4-9; Gigg D4-9; Gindles D4-9; Golborne KYZ5-9,YZ4, R4; Haigh B5-7*,YZ4-9,R4; Halliwell YZ4,Y5678, B4-9; Hardshaw R4; Harwood (Bolton) B4-9,A45, YZ4; Haughton U4-8,M457; Haulgh B4-9,YZ4,A45; Hawkshaw D4-9; Hazlehurst S4-9; Heap D4-8, H4-7,9,B4*; Gt and Lit Heaton D4,6-9; Heaton (Bolton) B4-9,YZ4-5,Y67; Heap D4-9; Helmshore pt D5-9; Heywood D4-9,H9,HQ4-8,B4,P4-9; Hindley YZ4-9; Holcombe D4-9; Hollins D4-9; Holme R5; Hooley Bridge H9; Hopwood D4-9,H5-9; Horwich B4-9,YZ459; Houghton W5-8; Y4,6-9,Z4-9; Houghton with Middleton and Arbury Y4-8; Lit Houghton S7; Hulme Z4; Hulton (Lit, Mid, Over) B4-9,YZ4; Huntley Brook D4-9; Ince YZ4-9,R4,Z6; Irlam S4-9,M567; Irlam Moss S5; Irlams o'th' Height S47; Irwell Vale D4-9; Kearsley (excl. Ringley) B4-7; Kearsley B4-9,Z48,Y4; Kenyon Z4-9,Y4-9,R4,K5-8; Kenyon Fold D4-9; Langtree see Standish; Lathom Z6; Lees NN4-8; Leigh Union Workhouse K9; Lench D4-9; Gt Lever B4-9; Lit Lever B4-9,AZ4,Y4; Lilly Hill D4-9; Limefield D4-9; Littleborough P5,Q4; Lostock (Bolton) B4-9,YZ459,A4; Lostock (Salford) S4-8, K9,YZ459; Lowton R4,KYZ4-9; Manchester (parish) M4-8; Marland Workhouse Q4; Mellor A45,L4; Middleton (nr Manchester) Q4-8,N4-9,D4, Z4-7,9,Y4,9; Milnrow P4-9; Monton S4-9,M567; Moorside S4-8; Mossley U4-9; Musbury D5-9; Nailors Green D4-9; Newchurch Q4; Newtown (Eccles) S47; Nuttall D4-9; Oldham NN4-9; Orrell (nr Wigan) YZ4-8,R4; Patricroft S4-9; Parr J5,R4-7; Peel Green S5; Pemberton YZ4-9,R4; Pendlebury Z4-8,S4,6-9; Pendleton S4,6-9,M67; Pennington KYZ4-9; Pigslee D4-9; Pilkington B4-9*,D4-9,B8*; Pilsworth D4-9,H5-9; Prestwich D46-9,M678; Radcliffe D4-9,B58*,P4-9; Ramsbottom DP4-9; Reddish M4; Redvales D4-9; Rhodes N4(pt),8,9 D4; Rhodes D4-9; Ringley D4-9,B4-9; Rochdale Q4-8, P4-7(pt),8; Roe Green S4-9; Royton NN4-9,D4, N8,9(pt); Rumworth B4-9,YZ4; Saddleworth NN4-9, Q4,7 (Yorks); Salford S4-9,M67(pt); Gt Sankey J4, R45,YZ5,W67; Scout D4-9; Sedgley D4,6-9; Sharples B4-9,Y4; Shaw D4; Shevington B5*,YZ4-9, E4; Shoresworth S4; Shuttleworth D4-9, B5; Simister D4,6-9; Simpson's Clough H9; Slattocks H9; Smithills (Halliwell) B4-9 Spotland P4-8,Q4; Spotland (Nearside) Q5-9; Spotland (Furtherside) Q5689; Stand D4-9; Standish B5*; Standish with Langtree Z4-9,Y4-7,E4,Y8; Stretford (pt) M4-7; Stubbins D4-9; Summerseat DP4-9; Swinton S4-9, Z4; Thornham D4,N9; Todmorden incl Walsden Q457; Todmorden and Langfield Q6; Tonge (Bolton) B4-9,YZ4; Tonge (Oldham) A4,N6789; Tonge A45; Tottington DP4-9,B4*; Tottington Higher End B4,P587; Trafford Park S5; Turn D4-9;

Turton B4-9, YZ4; Tyldesley KYZ4-9; Unsworth B4-9*,D4-9; Uppermill (Saddleworth) Q56; Urmston M567; Walkden S4-9; Walmsley D4-8,B4*; Walmersley B4,DP4-9; Walshaw pt D4-9; Wardley S4-9; Wardleworth Q4-9; Welch Whittle YZ4; Westhoughton B4-9,K9,YZ4-9; West Leigh KYZ4-9, X4-8,N4-7; Wham D4-9; Whitefield D4-9,B4-9*; Whitelees P65; Whittle D4-9; Whittleswick S7; Whitworth and Brandwood Q5-9; Wigan YZ4-8; Winstanley YZ4-9,R46; Winton S4-9,M57; Winwick-with-Hulme K6,YZ4-9; Wolstenholme P4-8; Woodhouses M78; Worsley S4-9; Worthington Y4-9,S458,E4; Wuerdle and Wardle Q4-9; Wythenshawe M4-7.

Indexed transcripts: Irlam, Cadishead, Rixton, Glazebrook, Hollins Green, 41-71, at Salford Local History Library.

Street Indexes (to areas held) at libraries at Bolton, Bury, Leigh, Manchester, Salford, Tameside/Stalybridge and Wigan.

Publications: *Tracing your Ancestors in Bolton*, 2nd edn., 1984; *Routes: A Guide to Family History in the Bury Area*. These list full details of all places and years held on census mf at Bolton and Bury Libraries.
Also list available of publications from The Secretary, Manchester & Lancs FHS, Clayton House, 59 Piccadilly, Manchester M1 2AQ.
Indexes: See *Marriage, Census and Other Indexes* for details of FHS indexes.
  Salford Local History Library has surname index 41-91 to Clifton, Swinton, Pendlebury.

MERSEYSIDE (post-1974 county) (key above)

See *Guide to Liverpool's Enumeration Districts in the 1851 Census*, Peter Park (Liverpool & Dist. FHS); £2.30 + p&p each vol. J.D.Griffiths, 9 Manor Rd, Lymm, Cheshire WA13 0AY.

Ainsdale J9;T4-9,O56; Aigburth KK4-9; Aintree F478,J5;KK4589; LY4; Allerton L4-7,J4578,KK4-9; OC4; Lit Altcar KK5; T4-9,L4,J45,O56; Appleby J7; Appleton KK5; Aughton KK4; Banks J5; Billinge RY4-8,J5,O56; Bickerstaffe J5-9,KK4; Birkdale T4-9,J59; Blowick T58,OJ5; Blundellsands KK9; Bold R4-8,J457-9,KK589,X567; Bootle C4-8, J456,7(pt)8,KK4-9; Buckley Hill KK9; Chadwick P4-7; Childwall L4-7,OC4,J458,KK4-9, R8; Churchtown (nr Southport) T4-9,J5,O56; Cronton J4-9,KK589,R4578,X567; Gt Crosby F4-8,KK45689, L456,Y4,J5; Lit Crosby F4-8,J5, KK4589,L45,Y4; Crossens T4-9,J5,O56; Croxteth Park J45,KK4-9, L4-7; Delph KK9; Ditton 589; Downholland J59; Eccleston (Prescot) J4-9,67, KK589,R4-8; Edge Hill J8; Everton KK4-9,L4-7,C4, J48; Farnworth J79, KK589; Fazakerley LJ4-7, C567,J4-7,KK4-9; Ford L45,KK4589,Y4,F578,J5; Formby T4-9,J459,KK4, L45,O56; Garston L4-7, OC4,J458,KK4-9; Hale J4-9,KK4-9,R8; Halewood J,4-9,KK4-9,L4-7,OC4,R8; Halsnead KK9; Halsall J59,KK4; Haydock R4-8,W56,YZ4-9; Hightown F478,KK9;

Lancashire (Merseyside) continued

Homer Green F5-8,KK9; Hough Green KK9; Huyton J4-9,KK4-9, L4-7,R8; Ince Blundell F4-8,KK45689,L45,Y4,J5; Kirby J57-9,L457,C578; Kirkby J6,KK457-9; Kirkdale L4-7,J48,KK4-9,C4; Kirkwood J4; Knowsley J4-9,KK5789,L5,R8; Lady's Green KK9; Lane End KK9; Leeds & Liverpool Canal (between Stanley and Derby wards) J7; Linacre see Bootle; Litherland KK45689,L456,O45, F4578,Y4,J5; Little Britain KK9; Liverpool L4-8,J59, KK4-9,K58; Liverpool Borough Prison J7; Liverpool Seamen's Orphan Inst. J8; Lunt F4578,KK4589,L45, J5; Lunts Heath J7; Lydiate O456,J5; Maghull O456, J5; Marshside T4-9,O56,J5; Melling (nr Ormskirk) O456,J5-9,T8; Moss Bank KK9; Netherton KK4589, L45,Y4,F57,J5; Newton-in-Makerfield (Newton-le-Willows) K5,Z4-9,R48,Y5-9,W56; North Meols O456,J5; Orrell (Bootle) KK45689,YZ4-9,F57; Orrell and Ford J5; Y4, Parr J4,KK589,R8; Penketh J4; W5-8, YZ5; Prescot L8,JR4-9,KK589; Prescott Union J7; Prescott Union Workhouse J89; Rainford KK589,R4-8,J49; Rainhill J5-9,KK589,R4-8; Rainhill & Rainhill Hospital J9; Ravenmeols O56,T68; Roby J4-9,L5,R8; Gt. Sankey J4; Scotland Ward J8; St. Helens KK589,R4-7,J9; Seaforth F4578,KK69; Sefton or Sephton F4-8,KK4589,L45,Y4,J5; Shipping J7; Simonswood J4-9,KK4,L4,O56,T8; Southport T4-9,O56,J59; Speke J4-9,KK4-9,OL4, R8; Sutton R4-8,J4,KK589,W5; Tarbock J4-9, KK5789,L5,R8; Thingwall J4-7,KK89; Thornton (Sefton) F4-8,KK45689,L45,Y4,J5; Toxteth Park KK4-9,L4-8,J8; Upton KK9; Vauxhall Ward J8; Walton J8; Walton-on-the-Hill CL4-7,J45,KK4-9; Waterloo F4-8,KK569,L7; Wavertree L4-7,J458, KK4-9,O4; West Derby (district) KK4-9,L4-8,J5; West Derby Union J7; Whiston J4-9,KK589; R4-8, Windle R4-8,J4,KK589; Lit and Much Woolton L4-7, J45,KK4-9,R8.

CHESHIRE (parishes formerly in Lancashire)

Cheshire Record Office.
41-91: complete area (Warrington, Winwick, Croft with Southworth, Prescot (part, Cuerdley, Penketh and Gt Sankey), Farnworth, Hale, Newchurch (part, Culcheth), Widnes).

Warrington Library (Cheshire Libraries and Museums Service).
Astbury 51-61; Astley 81; Bedford (Leigh) 61-81; Burtonwood 41-81; Collins Green 41-81; Croft 51-81; Cuerdley 51-81; Culcheth 61-81; Glazebury 81; Haydock 51,61; Houghton 51-81; Leigh (pt) 71; Newton in Makerfield (Newton-le-Willows) 51,61; Penketh 51-81; Poulton with Fearnhead 41-81 (incl. Padgate; Rixton with Glazebrook (including Hollinsgreen) 41-81; Winwick with Hulme 51-81; Woolston with Martinscroft 41-81.
91: complete pre and post 1974 **county**.
Also Great Sankey (Ches) 51-81.
Street indexes: Warrington Borough 41-81.
Note. The library does not hold Sutton in Merseyside 51.

Widnes Library.
41-91: Local area.

Other libraries (J = Knowsley; KK = Liverpool Record Office; M = Middleton; R = St Helens; W = Warrington; Y = Wigan Heritage Services History Shop; Z = Wigan Archives).
Appleton R41, J71; Burtonwood RY51,YZ51; Croft (nr Warrington) YZ41-81, R41,51; Cuerdley J41, YZ51; Ditton J41-91, R51,71,81; Houghton R41; Middleton (nr Warrington) Z41-81; Poulton with Fernhead W41,71; Southworth Z41-81, Y41-71, R41; Upton (Widnes) J71,KK91; Widnes K K51,81,91,R41-61,81, J41-91; Winwick with Hulme YZ 41-81, R41,51, M71.

LEICESTERSHIRE

Census Indexes and Publications:
  See *Marriage, Census and Other Indexes* for
Leicestershire & Rutland FHS 1851 census
transcript project and published indexes.
  See also Leicestershire R.O. below.

Leicestershire Record Office, Wigston Magna.
41-91: whole county (incl. city of Leicester and
district of Rutland). Indexes to parishes, to Leicester
public houses and streets.
Index 51: Includes much of the county, prepared by
Leics. & Rutland FHS.
81: Index for Leicestershire and Rutland (Mormon).
Note. Holdings formerly at the *Leicestershire
Libraries Information Centre* have been transferred
to the Record Office.

Loughborough University Library.
41-81: whole county.

Derbyshire County Library, Matlock.
41: Anstey, Cropston, Dishley, Shepshed,
Swithland, Thurcaston, Ulverscroft, Wanlip, Long
Whatton.
41-91: Parishes bordering on Derbys., including,
81: Albert, Appleby, Ashby de la Zouch,
Backthorpe, Bardon, Bardon Hill, Blackfordby,
Brand, Breedon, Castle Donington, Cavendish
Bridge, Coalville, Coleorton, Diseworth, Donington,
Donisthorpe, Gelsmoor, Griffydam, Heather,
Hedgefield, Hemington, Hugglescote, Kegworth,
Kingston on Soar, Lockington, Measham, Moira,
Newbold, Newton Burgoland and Netherscote,
Normanton le Heath, Oakthorpe, Osgathorpe,
Outworth, Packington, Ratcliffe on Soar,
Ravenstone, Settleworth, Smisby, Snareston,
Snibston, Staunton Harold, Stretton en le Field,
Swannington, Swepstone, Thringstone, Tonge,
Whitwick, Willesley, Wilson, Worthington.

Derby Central Library.
Appleby 41-91; Ashby de la Zouch 51-91; Bardon
81; Bardon Hill 81; Bardon Park 71; Blackfordby
51,61,81,91; Boothorpe 51; Breedon 51,71,81;
Breedon on the Hill 51,61,91; Bromley Hurst 51;
Castle Donington 51-91; Cavendish Bridge
51,81,91; Chilcote 41-71; Coalville 51,81; Coleorton
51-81; Diseworth 51-91; Donnington-le-Heath
51,61; Donisthorpe 41,51,61,81,91, Griffydam
81,91; Heather 51-91; Hemington 51-91;
Hugglescote 51-81; Isley Walton 61; Kegworth
51-91; Langley Priory 51,61,71,91; Littleworth 91;
Lockington 51-91; Lount 91; Measham 41-91;
Newton Burgoland 51-91; Newton Nethercote 51-
91; Normanton-en-le-Heath 51-91; Oakthorpe
41-91; Osgathorpe 51-91; Packington 41-81;
Ravenstone 41-81; Snareston 51-9; Snibston
Packington 51,81; Staunton Harold 51-91; Stone
Rows 61; Stretton-le-Field 41-91; Swannington
51,61,81; Swepstone 51-91; Thringstone 51,61,81;
Tongue 81,91; Whitwick 51,61,81; Willesley 41-91;
Wilson 61-91; Worthington 51-91.

Northamptonshire Record Office.
81 only unless shown otherwise: Bittesby; Blaston;
Gt Bowden; Bringhurst; Claybrook; Cranow;
Drayton; Gt Easton; Fleckney; Foxton; Gumley;
Hallaton; Holt; Horninghold; Husbands Bosworth;
51,81; Kibworth Beauchamp and Harcourt;
Knaptoft; E and W Langton; Laughton; Lubenham;
Market Harborough 71,81; Medbourne; Mowsley;
Othorpe; Peatling Magna and Parva; Saddington;
Shangton; Shearsby; Slawston; Smeeton Westerby;
Stanford; Stockerston 71 only; Stonton Eyville;
Swinford; Theddingworth; Thorpe Langton;
Turlangton; Wigston Parva; Willoughby Waterless.

Nottinghamshire County Library, Nottingham.
51,81: Barkestone, Plungar.

Nottingham University Library.
51-91: Some parishes bordering on
Nottinghamshire and Derbyshire.

Staffordshire Record Office, Stafford.
Chilcote 61,71; Coton in the Elms 51,61,81.

Burton upon Trent (Staffs.) Library.
41: Appleby, Chilcote, Measham, Packington,
Ravenstone, Stretton-en-le-Field.

Warwickshire Record Office, Warwick.
51,81,91 only unless shown otherwise: Arnesby;
Ashby Magna and Parva; Aston Flamville (not 91);
Atterton 51,61,91; Barwell 51 only; Bittesby 91;
Bitteswell; Broughton Astley; Bruntingthorpe;
Burbage (Not 91); Catthorpe; Claybrooke Magna
and Parva; Cottesbach; Drayton Fenny (51-91);
Dunton Bassett; Earl Shilton 51 only; Elmsthorpe 51
only; Frolesworth; Gilmorton; Higham-on-the-Hill 51
only; Hinckley 51 and 81; N and S Kilworth 51,91
only; Kimcote 51 only; Kimcote in Walton 51 only;
Knaptoft; Leire 51 only; Kimcote 51,91; Kimcote in
Walton 51 only; Knaptoft; Leire 51,91; Lutterworth
51,91 only; Misterton 51,91 only; Peatling Magna;
Parva 51,81; Ratcliffe Culey 51-91; Sapcote 51,81;
Sharnford 51,81; Shawell; Shearsby; Sheepy
Magna and Parva 51-91; Starmore see Westrill;
Stoke Golding 51 only; Stoney Stanton 51,81;
Swinford; Ullesthorpe; Walton in Knaptoft 51,91
only; Welford 51,91; Westrill 51,61 only; Wigston
Parva 51,91 only; Willoughby Waterless; Witherley
51-91.

Birmingham Central Library (Local Studies).
Fenny Drayton 51.

LINCOLNSHIRE
Northern border now in Humberside.

Census Indexes and Publications:
See *Marriage, Census and Other Indexes* for the extensive series of census indexes (1851, 1871 and 1881) complete county published by Lincolnshire FHS.
Lincolnshire Returns of the Census of Worship 1851, ed R.W. Ambler, Lincolnshire Record Society **72**, 1979.

Lincoln Central Reference Library.
41-91: whole county.

Lincolnshire Archives Office, Lincoln.
51,81,91: For the whole of the historic county of **Lincolnshire**, including those areas included in out-of-county registration districts (e.g. Swinderby in Newark RD).
41-71: Lincoln city (photocopies).

Grimsby Central Library
41: North-east Lincolnshire; also Boston 61,71; Caistor 51-71; Glanford Brigg (excl. Winterton) 51-71; Louth 51-71.
81: Caistor, Gainsborough, Glanford, Horncastle, Lincoln, Louth, Spilsby RDs.
91: Spilsby, Horncastle, Louth, Glanford Brigg, Caistor, Gainsborough, Isle of Axholme, Lincoln.

Gainsborough Library.
41-71: Gainsborough (local government area as at the time; bound photocopies indexed by streets and occupations). Corringham (incl. Gt and Lit Corringham, Aisby, Dunstall, Huckerby, Somerby and Yawthorpe) 41-61; E Stockwith 41-61; Heapham 41-61; Lea 41-71; Marton (nr Gainsborough) 41; Morton (nr Gainsborough) 41-71; Walkerith 41-61.
81: Gainsborough and Glandford Brigg (part) RDs.
91: Gainsborough and area.

Grantham Library.
41-91: Grantham and Spitalgate.

Horncastle Library.
81: Horncastle.
91: Horncastle and area.

Louth Library.
41-91: East Lindsey (parts around Louth).

Scunthorpe Central Library
51,81,91: Caistor (76 parishes); Gainsborough (49 parishes); Glanford Brigg (50 parishes). Also Goole and Thorne Lincs and Yorkshire parishes.
41: most of the 41 returns are held but it is advisable to check first on the availablity of the individual returns and the microfilm reader.

Sleaford Library.
41-91: Sleaford Area; Skegness and areas.

Spalding Library.
41-91: Spalding.

Stamford Library:
41-91: Stamford.

Bishop Grosseteste College, Lincoln.
51: Lincoln (city) (photocopy; some sections now illegible through age).

Doncaster Central Library (South Yorkshire).
Belton 51,81; Crowle 51,81; Eastoft 51,81; Epworth 51,81; E and W Hardwick 41,81; Keadby 51,81; Wroor 51,81.

County Record Office, Huntingdon, Cambridgeshire.
51-91: Barholm; Braceborough; Crowland; Greatford; Stamford; Stowe; Tallington; Uffington; West Deeping; Wilsthorpe.

Peterborough Library (Cambs. C.C.)
51-91: Barholme; Braceborough; Greatford; Stamford; Stowe; Tallington; Uffington; West Deeping; Wilsthorpe.
41-91: Crowland (Peterborough RD).

Northamptonshire Record Office, Northampton.
71,81: Barholm; Braceborough; Casewick 81 only; Crowland 51 also; W Deeping; Greatford; Stamford St Mary; Stamford All SS, St. Martin, Workhouse 71 only; Stamford St. John, St. Michael 81 only; Stowe
81 only: Tallington; Uffington; Wilsthorpe.

Leicestershire Record Office, Wigston Magna.
41-81: Lincolnshire parishes bordering Leicestershire and Rutland.

Nottinghamshire County Library, Nottingham.
51,81 (probably **91** also): Barkston, Bassingham, Beckingham, Brant Broughton, Carlton-le-Moorland, Caythorpe, Claypole, Dry Doddington, Fenton, Fulbeck, Hougham, Marston Syston, Norton Disney, N Scarle, Stapleford, Stragglethorpe, Stubton, Swinderby.
81 only: Allington, Beckingham Sutton, Beckingham Grange, Foston, Long Bennington, Sedgebrook, Suston, Thurlby, Westborough.

Nottinghamshire Archives, Nottingham.
41-91: as *Nottinghamshire County Library.*

Nottingham University Library.
51-91: A few parishes bordering on Notts.

Sheffield Central Library (Local Studies).
81: Crowle, Epworth.

Sheffield Record Office.
51: Althorpe, Amcotts, Belton, Crowle, Eastoft, Epworth, Keadby, Wroot.

LONDON

Note. The places in this section are arranged according to the county in which they formerly lay.

Census Indexes and Publications:
For FHS publications of indexes to **1851** for the whole metropolis, see *Lists of Londoners* (2nd ed., 1997). Repositories should have copies at least of their own area. For other FHS projects, see *Marriage, Census and Other Indexes*.
For library held indexes, see below.

City of London
This is a small entity in the very centre of London, and does not include the large outer parishes of Stepney, Holborn, Lambeth, Westminster etc.

Guildhall Library, London EC2P 2EJ.
41,61,71,81,91: City of London.
51: City of London plus district of St. Peter, Saffron Hill.
41: parts of Strand Dist., Lincolns Inn.
41-91: Inner and Middle Temple.
41 (part), 51-61, 81-91: Liberty of the Rolls.
Card Index from names of parish or extra parochial places to reel number, 1841-1871.
City of London street indexes compiled by PRO, 1841-71, by OPCS 1881-91.

North-west London, formerly Middlesex.
See also under Middlesex, for present LBs of Barnet, Brent, Ealing, Enfield, Haringey, Harrow, Hillingdon and Hounslow.

City of Westminster Archives Centre, 10 St. Ann's Street, London SW1P 2XR.
41-91: Westminster (pre-1965 city), with street indexes.
41-91: St.Marylebone.
51-91: Paddington (including Queen's Park). with street indexes.

Kensington Central Library, Phillimore Walk, London W8 7RX
41-91: Kensington (area of old borough).
Some returns are incomplete, and some (for 61) are at *Chelsea Library* (below). Ecclesiastical census, Kensington RD, indexes by church name. Indexes for street and house names.
51: Surname index on microfiche.

Chelsea Library, Kings Road, SW3 5ED.
41-91: Chelsea (area of old borough).
Some returns are incomplete, and some are at *Kensington Library* (above).
Indexes for street and house names.

Hammersmith and Fulham Archives & Local History Centre, The Lilla Huset, 191 Talgarth Rd, W6 8BJ.
41-91: Fulham, Hammersmith.

Camden Local Studies Library, Holborn Library, 32-38 Theobalds Road, London WC1X 8PA.
41-91: Hampstead, Holborn, St. Pancras (former boroughs).

Finsbury Library, 245 St. John Street, EC1 V4.
91: Census returns for the Finsbury local area.

Islington Central Reference Library, 2 Fieldway Crescent, London N5 1PF.
41-91: Islington (61 excl. E. Islington, Dist.145, missing at PRO); Finsbury (St. Luke only).

Hackney Archives Department, 43 De Beauvoir Road, London N1 5SQ.
41-91: Hackney, Shoreditch, Stoke, Newington; incl. those parts of the former district of South Hornsey that were detached from Hornsey proper, being part of or adjacent to Stoke Newington.

Tower Hamlets Local History Library and Archives, Bancroft Library, 277 Bancroft Rd, London E1 4DQ.
41-91: Bethnal Green, Mile End Old Town, Poplar, St. George's-in-East, Stepney, Whitechapel (RDs now in LB of Tower Hamlets).

North-east London, formerly Essex.
See under Essex, for present LBs of Havering, Newham, Redbridge and Waltham Forest.

South-east London, formerly Kent.
See also under Kent for present LBs of Bexley and Bromley.

Greenwich Local History Library, Woodlands, 90 Mycenae Road, Blackheath, SE3 7SE.
41: Deptford (St. Nicholas), Woolwich, Greenwich, Charlton, Eltham, Mottingham, Kidbrooke, Plumstead.
51: As above but excl. Mottingham and incl. Lewisham.
61,81: As 41, excl. Mottingham, Lewisham; incl. Blackheath (All SS).
71: As above but excl. Blackheath.
91: Deptford (St. Nicholas), Greenwich, Eltham, Lewisham (part), Lee, Charlton, Kidbrooke, Plumstead, Woolwich, Orpington, St. Paul's Cray, Mottinghan, Farnborough.
Indexes: Mostly street indexed.
41: Surnames for Plumstead, Eltham, Kidbrooke, St. Nicholas Deptford.
91: Street indexed except Lewisham, Orpington, St. Paul's Cray and Farnborough.

Lewisham Local Studies Centre, Lewisham Library, 199-201 Lewisham High Street, London SE13 6LG.
41-91: Lewisham (covering SDs of Lee, Sydenham and Lewisham village); **Deptford St. Paul**.
41,61,71,91: Deptford St. Nicholas (41-91 at Greenwich, see above).
Street indexes to all returns.

London continued

South-west London, formerly Surrey.
  See also under Surrey for present LBs of
Croydon, Kingston, Merton, Richmond, Sutton.

*Southwark Local Studies Library, 211 Borough High
Street, SE1 1JA*
41-91: LB of Southwark; each year street indexed.
Surname indexes. Readers with a precise address
(including street number) may order copies from the
surname indexes at £6 per year:
41: Christ Church.
51: Christ Church, St. Saviour, St. Olave, St. Mary
Magdalen Bermondsey, St. George the Martyr,
St. Giles Camberwell, St. John Horselydown, St.
Thomas, St. Mary Newington, St. Mary Rotherhithe.
61: Christ Church, St. Thomas, St. Saviour.
71: St. Olave, St. James Bermondsey sub-district.
81: St.George the Martyr (part).

*Lambeth Archives Department, Minet Library,
52 Knatchbull Road, SE5 9QY.*
41-91: Lambeth, Clapham and **Streatham**
(comprising present LB of Lambeth).
51: Also in photocopy bound volumes. Street
indexes 41-81. Trades index 41.

*Battersea Library (Wandsworth LH Collection),
265 Lavender Hill SW11 1JB.*
41-91: Battersea, Putney, Streatham, Tooting
Graveney and Wandsworth.
91: only for Clapham.
  *Putney 1851. A survey based on the Census
Returns* (Wandsworth Hist. Soc.).

MIDDLESEX
Now part of Greater London. See 'London', above,
for present LBs of Camden, Hackney,
Hammersmith, Islington, Kensington and Chelsea,
Tower Hamlets and City of Westminster, formerly in
Middlesex.

Census Indexes and Publications:
  For library held indexes, see below.
  For FHS publications of indexes to **1851** for the
whole metropolis, see *Lists of Londoners* (2nd ed.,
1997). Repositories should have copies at least of
their own area. For other FHS projects, see
Marriage, Census and Other Indexes.

*Enfield Library, Civic Centre, Silver Street, Enfield,
Middlesex, EN1 3XJ*
41-91: Enfield and Edmonton.
Surname indexes: 51,71,91. Enfield and
Edmonton; **41-91:** Street guide to enumeration
districts Enfield and Edmonton.

*LB of Barnet, Archives and Local Studies Centre,
Hendon Library, The Burroughs, Hendon NW4 4BQ.*
41-91: present LB of Barnet: in Middlesex.,
Edgware, Finchley, Friern Barnet, Hendon, Monken
Hadley.

Middlesex continued

Hertfordshire County Library, Hertford.
41-81: South Mimms.
51-81: Monken Hadley.

*Bruce Castle Museum (LB of Haringey), Lordship
Lane, N17 8NU.*
41 (incomplete)**, 51-81: Tottenham and Hornsey**
RDs.
91: Tottenham, Wood Green and Hornsey (not
indexed).
Index to families and independent persons (not
dependent wives and children) with occupations,
streets and places.

*Grange Museum of Local History (LB of Brent).
Neasden Lane, NW10 1QB.*
41-71: (photocopies): Kingsbury, Willesden,
Wembley portion of Harrow parish (RDs making up
what is now LB of Brent).
81 (mf): as above.
Checklist to name and place, 41.

Harrow Civic Centre Library.
41-91: Harrow (incl. Harrow Weald, Pinner,
Wembley). Edgware, Kingsbury, Gt. and Lt.
Stanmore.
41,51: Hendon.
51 only: Willesden.

Uxbridge Library (LB of Hillingdon).
41-91: LB of **Hillingdon** (approx. area comprising
Bedfont, Cowley, Cranford, West Drayton, Eastcote,
Harefield, Harlington, Harmondsworth, Hayes,
Hillingdon, Heathrow, Ickenham, Longford, Northolt,
Norwood, Ruislip, Southall, Uxbridge, Uxbridge
Moor, Yeading, Yiewsley).
41 incl. Brentford, Greenford, Hanwell, Northolt,
Perivale.
51 incl. Laleham, Littleton, Shepperton, Sunbury,
Hanworth, Feltham, Ashford, Staines, Stanwell.
71-91 incl. part of Staines.
Card index to surnames in progress.

*Ruislip Library (LB of Hillingdon), Bury Street,
Ruislip.*
51-71: LB of **Hillingdon** (approx. area, as at
Uxbridge Library but actual size photocopies).

*Ealing Local History Library, Central Library,
103 Ealing Broadway Centre, W5 5JY.*
41-81: Acton, Ealing (incl. Old Brentford) Gt.
Greenford, Hanwell, Northolt, Norwood Precinct
(incl Southall), Perivale, Twyford Abbey (West
Twyford).
41 only: Chiswick, Fulham, Cowley, Cranford, West
Drayton, Harefield, Harlington, Harmondsworth,
Hayes, Hillingdon, Ickenham, Ruislip (incl. Eastcote
and Northwood).
41-61 only: New Brentford.
91: as 41-81 but excluding Old Brentford.
Index: Northolt 51-71 individuals.

Middlesex continued

Hounslow Library, Treaty Road, Hounslow.
41-91: East Bedfont, Feltham, Hanworth, Cranford, Heston, Isleworth, (includes Hounslow), Old and New Brentford, Chiswick.

Chiswick Library (LB of Hounslow), Dukes Avenue, W4 2AB.
41-91: Old and New Brentford, Chiswick.

Feltham Library, High Street, Feltham.
41-81: East Bedfont, Feltham, Hanworth.

Twickenham District Library.
41,51: Twickenham parliamentary constituency covering Twickenham, Teddington, Hampton and Whitton.

Surrey Record Office, Woking (from mid-1998).
Ashford 41-81; Bedfont 41-81; Cranford 51-81; Feltham 41-81; Hampton 41,51; Hampton Wick 41,51; Hanworth 41-81; Harlington 51-81; Harmondsworth 51-81; Laleham 41-81; Littleton 41-81; Shepperton 41-81; Staines 41,51,71,81; Stanwell 41,51,71,81; Sunbury 41-81; Teddington 41,51.

MONMOUTHSHIRE
See with WALES.

NORFOLK

Census Indexes and Publications:
See *Marriage, Census and Other Indexes* for Norfolk & Norwich FHS publications, Norwich 1851.

Norwich Central Library.
41-91: Norfolk and Norwich.

Norfolk Record Office, Norwich.
41,51: Beetley, East Bilney.

Great Yarmouth Library.
41-91: Census returns are available for the Great Yarmouth and Gorleston area as far north as Winterton and Martham, and as far south as St.Olaves and Somerleyton (including Lowestoft).

Kings Lynn Library.
41-81: Kings Lynn

Thetford Library.
91: Thetford only.

Wisbech (Cambs.) Library.
41-91: adjacent parishes of West Norfolk, as asterisked under *Cambridgeshire Record Office.*
41 only: Wiggenhall St. German's, St. Mary Magdalen, St. Mary the Virgin and St. Peter's.

Norfolk continued

County Record Office, Cambridge.
(**61:** places are also at *Huntingdon R.O.*; asterisked places also 41-91 at *Wisbech Library.*)
41: Clenchwarton; Emneth; North Lynn St Edmunds; Terrington St. Clement; Terrington St. John; Tilney All Saints; Tilney-cum-Islington; Tilney St Lawrence; Walpole St. Andrew; Walpole St. Peter; Walsoken; West Walton; Wiggenhall St. Germans; Wiggenhall St. Mary Magdalene; Wiggenhall St Mary the Virgin; Wiggenhall St. Peter.
Bexwell 71,91; Clenchwarton* 41-91; Crimplesham 61; Denver 71,91; W Dereham 51; Downham Market 91; Emneth* 41-91; Fordham 71; Hilgay 61(pt)-91; Outwell* 51-91; Roxham 71,91; Roxham 71,91; Ryston 71,91; The Smeeth 51-91; Southery 61,91; Stradsett (pt) 51; Terrington St Clement* and St John* 41-91; Tilney All SS*, St Lawrence* and cum-Islington* 41-91; Tilney St.John 51,71; Upwell* 51-91; Walpole St Andrew* and St Peter* 41-91; Walsoken* 41-91; W Walton* 51-91; Welney 51-91.
Transcript and index, 51: Outwell, Upwell, Walsoken, Welney.

Suffolk Record Office, Bury St. Edmunds.
41: Clavering Hundred.
51-91: Norfolk parishes bordering Suffolk.

Suffolk Record Office, Lowestoft.
51-91: Norfolk parishes bordering Suffolk.

NORTHAMPTONSHIRE
Soke of Peterborough now in Cambridgeshire.

See *Genealogical Sources in Cambridgeshire*, Cambs RO, 2nd edition, 1994, for details of census mf for 41-91 for parishes in Soke of Peterborough.

Census Indexes and Publications:
See *Marriage, Census and Other Indexes* for Northamptonshire and Peterborough FHS 1851 census index projects and publications.
1851 Religious Census to be published by Northamptonshire Record Society.

Northamptonshire Record Office, Northampton.
41,51,71,81: Northamptonshire incl. the Soke of Peterborough.
61: Northampton RD.
91: arranged by registration district which corresponds to poor law union microfiche.
Street indexes to Northampton 51,71,81,91.
Street Indexes for Kettering 91.
Street Indexes for Peterborough 1881

Northampton Central Library.
61: Northamptonshire.

Northamptonshire continued

Buckinghamshire County Reference Library, Aylesbury.
41-91: some parishes in Brackley and Potterspury areas bordering Buckinghamshire.

Centre for Oxon Studies, Oxford Central Library.
51-81: Appletree (not 61), Aston le Walls, Lr and Upr Boddington, Chacombe, Chipping Warden, Edgcote, Grimsbury (Banbury) (also 41), Middleton Cheney, Warkworth.
81 only: Astrop, Aynho, Brackley (and Union Workhouse), Charlton, Croughton, Evenley, Hinton, Kings Sutton, Newbottle, Steane, Turweston, Westbury, Whitfield.
91: whole county.

Banbury Library (Oxon C.C.).
51-91: Banbury RD: SDs of Banbury and Cropredy; Brackley RD/SD. Probably as for *Oxford Central Library* above.

Bedfordshire Record Office, Bedford.
Higham Park 61-91; Higham Ferrers 61,91; Irchester 61; Irthlingborough 61,+91; Newton Bromswold 61-91; Rushden 61-81.

Leicestershire Record Office, Wigston Magna.
41-91: Northamptonshire parishes bordering on Leicestershire and Rutland.

Cambridgeshire Record Office, Cambridge.
Eye (pt) 51; Peterborough 61; Peterborough Minster Precincts, St Mary (pt) 71.

Cambridgeshire County Record Office, Huntingdon.
41-91: All parishes in Soke of Peterborough (amalgamated 1965 with Hunts. comprises of Ailsworth; Ashton; Bainton; Barnack; Borough Fen; Castor; Deeping Gate; Elton; Eye; Glinton; Gunthorpe; Helpston; Marsholm; Maxey; Newborough; Northborough; Paston; Peterborough; Peakirk; St. Martin; Stamford Baron; Sutton; Thornhaugh; Ufford; Upton; Walton; Wansford; Werrington; Wittering and Wothorpe), Collyweston; Easton-on-the-Hill; Hemington (not 71); Luddington (not 71); Lutton (not 51); Thurning and Winwick.
41,61,81-91: Barnwell St.Andrew, Cotterstock; Fotheringay; Dundle; Polebrook; Southwick; Tansor; Warmington.
41,61,91: Apethorpe; Duddington; Glapthorne; Nassington; Yarwell.
41 only: Benefield; Northampton.
51-61, 81-91: Chelveston, Stanwick.
61,81-91: Barnwell All Saints; Danford; Hargrave; Lilford; Pilton; Raunds; Ringstead; Stoke Doyle; Thorpe Achurch; Wadenhoe.
Transcripts index 51: Peterborough.
Indexed transcripts for Clapton; Etton; Luddington; Lutton; Thurning; Titchmarsh; Wansford; Winwick and all parishes in Raunds sub-district.
81: Hunts FHS surname index for Oundle and Thrapston districts.

Peterborough Library (Cambs. C.C.).
Oundle Reg. Dist. 41-81: Apethorpe 51-71; Armston 51; Ashton 51,61; Barnwell 51; Benefield Upper and Lower 51,61; Blatherwick 51,61; Bulwick 51,61; Cotterstock 51-81; Deene 51,61; Deenthorpe 51,61; Fotheringhay 51-81; Glapthorne 51-71; Hemington 51, Kings Cliffe 51-71; Lilford 51; Luddington 51; Lutton 51; Nassington 51-71; Oundle 51,61; Pilton 51; Polebrook 51; Southwick 51-81; Stoke Doyle 51; Tansor 51-81; Thorpe Achurch 51; Wadenhoe 51; Warmington 51-81; Gt. and Lt. Weldon 51,61; Wigsthorpe 51; Wood Newton 51-71; Yarwell 51-71; Yarwell 61,71.
Stamford Reg. Dist. 41-91 unless stated: Ashton; Bainton; Barnack; Collyweston (not 41); Duddington (not 41,61,71); Easton-on-the-Hill (not 41); Pilsgate; Southorpe; Stamford St. Martin's; Thornhaugh; Ufford; Wansford; Wittering; Wothorpe.
Peterborough Reg.Dist. 41-91: Ailsworth; Borough Fen; Castor; Deeping Gate; Etton; Eye; Glinton; Gunthorpe; Helpston; Longthorpe; Marholm; Maxey; Newborough; Northborough; Paston; Peakirk; Peterborough and hamlets; Sutton; Upton; Walton; Werrington.
Surname Index 51: Peterborough St John Baptist (incl. Dogsthorpe, Eastfield, Longthorpe, Newark).

Lincolnshire Record Office, Lincoln.
91: Ashton (in Ufford); Bainton; Bornack; Collyweston; Duddington; Easton-on-the-Hill; Pilsgate (in Barnack); Southorpe; Stamford Baron; Thornhaugh; Ufford; Wansford; Wittering; Wothorpe (in Stamford Baron).

Warwickshire Record Office, Warwick.
51-91 unless shown otherwise: Barby, Clay Coton (not 71), Crick, Elkington, Kilsby, Lilbourne, Onley (not 91), Stanford, Yelvertoft.
81 only: Aston le Walls, Lr and Upr Boddington.

Birmingham Central Library (Local Studies).
51: Kilsby.

NORTHUMBERLAND

South-east tip, incl. Newcastle-upon-Tyne, now in Tyne & Wear.

Census Indexes and Publications:
See *Marriage, Census and Other Indexes* for N'hmbd & Durham FHS 1851 census publications.

Morpeth Records Centre, The Kylins, Loandsdean.
41-71: whole (historic) **county.**
81, 91: Northumberland (post-1974, excl. Newcastle and S-E of old county, Tynemouth, Longbenton, Wallsend etc.).

Newcastle-upon-Tyne Central Library.
41-91: Newcastle-upon-Tyne (all areas within post-1974 city boundary, incl. Byker, Elswick, Fenham, Benwell and Jesmond); Street indexes.

Tyne and Wear Archives Dept., Blandford House, Blandford Square, Newcastle-upon-Tyne.
41-91: Tyne & Wear.

Durham County Council, Arts Libraries & Museums.
41-81: (post 74 county only). **91:** (historic County of Durham) divided between *Durham (city)* and *Darlington Libraries:*
Darlington, Teesdale and Sedgefield (pt), Union Districts at Darlington (plus southern parts historic County not now in Durham for 91).
Remainder at *Durham*.
41-91: Bishop Auckland only, also held at *Bishop Auckland Town Hall Library.*

Gateshead Libraries and Arts, Local Studies Depts.
Barlow 71, Barmston 51-81, Beamish 41,81, Bedlington 41, Biddick South 51, Bill Quay 81,91, Birtley 51-91, Bleach Green 71, North Blyth 41, Blaydon 51,71,81, Bolden 41, Broom 41, Burnmoor 51,81, Byers Green 41, Cambois 41, Chester-le-Street 51,81, Chester Moor 81, Choppington 41, Chopwell 41-91, Cocken 51,81, Coundon Grange 41, Crawcrook 41,51,61,71,91, Crookgate 71, Dunston 41-91, Edmondsley 81, Eighton Banks 81,91, Gateshead 41-91, Gateshead Fell 41,51, Low Fell 91, Fatfield 81, Felling 81,91, Harraton 51-81, Harton 41, Heworth 41-91, Hedworth 41, Jarrow 41, Kibblesworth 51,81,91, Lambton 51, Lamesley 41-91, Lintz Green 41, Lumbley Lt & Gt 51,81, Marley Hill 51,71-91, Monkton 41, Muggleswick 41, Ouston 41-81, Pelton 41-81, Pelton Fell 81, Plawsworth 41,51,81, Ravensworth 41, Ryton 41-91 Ryton Woodside 41,51,61, Tanfield 41, Team Colliery 81, Sacriston 81, Stanley 41, Stella 41-71,91, South Shields 41, Swalwell 71-91, Netherton 41, Sleekburn 41, Springwell 81,Swalwell 41,51,61 Urpeth 41,51,81, Usworth 51-81, Washington 51-81, Waldridge 41,51,81, Windy Nook 91, Winlaton 41-91, Whickham 41-91, Witton Gilbert 41,51,71,81, Woodside 71.

North Tyneside LS Centre, North Shields.
41-91: Easdon, Tynemouth, Longbenton, North Shields, Wallsend and area.

NOTTINGHAMSHIRE

Census Indexes and Publications:
See *Marriage, Census and Other Indexes* for Nottinghamshire FHS series of published indexes, 1851-1891.
Religion in Victorian Nottinghamshire: The Religious Census of 1851, 2 vols., Record Series of Centre for LH, University of Nottingham Dept. of Adult Education, **7**, 1988.

Nottinghamshire County Library, Local Studies Library, Nottingham.
41-91: whole county. Index to parishes in the county, and to streets in Nottingham (also Newark, Mansfield, Worksop, 81 only).

Nottinghamshire Archives, Nottingham.
41-91: whole county.
Index to parishes in county, streets in Nottingham.

Nottingham University Library.
41-91: whole county (excl. a few places but incl. Shardlow RD). Index to places 41-71 (reel only).

Broxtowe District Library, Beeston.
51-81: Broxtowe District.

Gedling District Library, Arnold.
51-71: Arnold (also 81), Burton Joyce, Calverton (also 81), Carlton (also 81), Colwick, Gedling, Lambley, Linby, Newstead, Papplewick, Stoke Bardolph, Woodborough.

Hucknall Library.
51-91: Hucknall and surrounding villages.

Kirkby-in-Ashfield Library.
51-91: Kirkby and surrounding villages.
81: Ashfield District.

Rushcliffe District Library, West Bridgford.
51-91: Rushcliffe District.
51 (transcripts; asterisked places also held at Bingham Library): Aslockton*, Bingham*, Car Colston, Colston Bassett*, Costock, Cotgrave, Cropwell Bishop* and Butler*, Edwalton, Hickling, Holme Pierrepont, Keyworth, Kinoulton, Langar* (incl. Barnston and Wiverton), E and W Leake, Normanton-on-Soar, Owthorpe* (incl. Lodge on the Wolds), Plumtree (incl. Normanton and Clipston), Radcliffe-on-Trent, Rempstone, Scarrington*, Shelford* (incl. Saxondale and Newton), Stanford-on-Soar, Stanton-on-the-Wolds, Sutton Bonington, Thorpe, Tythby*, Whatton*, Widmerpool, Willoughby-on-the-Wolds, Wysall.

Newark District Library.
51: Registration Districts 2134-38.
61: RDs 2470-76, 2478-81.
71: RDs 3532-39, 3541-44.
81: RDs 3368-79.

Newark Museum, Appletongate.
41-91: Census for Newark and Sherwood area. Notts FHS published indexes available.
Burgess Rolls of Newark Borough can be used as indexes.

Nottinghamshire continued

Mansfield Central Library.
51-81: Blidworth, Hucknall, Upr Langwith, Mansfield (also 41), Mansfield Woodhouse (also 41), Skegby, Sookholme (also 41, not 61), Sutton-in-Ashfield, Teversal, Warsop (also 41), Worksop (also 41, not 51).
61-81: Annesley, Brinsley, Carburton, Cuckney, Edwinstowe, Felley, Kirkby-in-Ashfield, Lambley, Linby, Moor Green, Newstead, Newthorpe, Norton, Osberton, Papplewick, Scofton, Selston, Underwood, Woodborough, Woodhouse (Hall).
61,81 only: Bathley, Bilsthorpe, Budby, Calverton, Caunton, Clipstone, Cromwell, Eakring, Eastwood, Kneesall, Maplebeck, N Muskham, Norwell, Norwell Woodhouse, Ollerton, Ompton, Perlethorpe, Rufford, Wellow (also 41).
  Also Greasley 61,71; Portland Row 71,81; Radford 61,71; Shireoaks 71,81; Tuxford 41,71; Welbeck 41,71,81; Wellow 41,61,81; Whiteborough 71,81, Whitwell 61,71.
  Also single years for many local places, mainly 71 but some 61 or 81.
91: Mansfield RD complete; Worksop RD (Worksop, Carburton SDs only); Basford RD (Greasley SD only); Southwell RD (Kneesall SD only).

Retford Library.
41-81: Bassetlaw area.
51 incl. whole of E Retford RD, ie Gringley, Clarborough, E Retford and Tuxford SDs; Carlton SD of Worksop RD; Misterton to W Burton parishes in Gainsborough RD; Misson and Finningley parishes in Doncaster RD.
81: Enumeration Districts 3299-3304.
91: Covers piece nos. 2633/38-42; 3867.

Sutton-in-Ashfield Library.
51-91: Ashfield District (except Hucknall & Torkard). Also **41:** Annesley, Annesley Woodhouse, Arnold, Attenborough, Chilwell, Felley, Hucknall Huthwaite and Torkard, Kirkby-in-Ashfield, Stapleford, Strelley, Toton, Trowell.
81-91: Mansfield district.

Worksop Library.
41-81: Worksop RD.

Leicestershire Record Office, Wigston Magna.
41-81: Notts. parishes bordering Leicestershire, incl. RDs of Melton and Loughborough; also 81 only, Bingham.

Lincoln Central Reference Library.
41-91: Notts. parishes bordering Lincs., incl. Gainsborough RD

Scunthorpe Central Library
51-91: Gainsborough RD (49 parishes). Many of the 1841 returns are also held but it is advisable to check availability before visiting.

Ilkeston Library (Dbys.).
41-91: Ainsworth; Cossall; Trowell.

Derbyshire County Library, Matlock.
41-91: Notts. parishes bordering Derbyshire, including; Annesley, Attenborough, Awsworth, Beggarlee, Bramcote, Brimsley, Chilliwell, Codnor, Cossall, Duncill, Eastwood, Fackley, Greasley, Hucknall, Kimberley, Kirby-in-Ashfield, Nuttall, Stapleford, Stoneyford, Toton, Trent College, Torwell, Watnall (Charnworth and Cantelupe), Whitborough, Woodlinkin.
41 only: Babworth, Ranby, Babworth Forest, Great Morton, Morton, Morton Grange, Little Morton, Bilby, Barnby, Blyth, Goldthorpe in Hodsock, Hodsock Park, Hodsock Woodhouse, Hodsock, Oldcoats, Norney in Styrrup, Styrrup, Torworth, Bothamsall, Boughton, North Carlton, Wigthorpe, South Carlton, North Carlton, Cuckney, Holbeck, Nether Langwith, Langwith Cotton Mill, Norton (practically unreadable), Habblesthorpe, Beckingham, Bole, West Burton, Clarborough, East Retford Union Workhouse, Bollom, Spittal Hill, Little Gringley, Moorgate, Wilham, Wiseton, Askham, Rockley, Beavercoates (unreadable), Bilsthorpe, Darlton, East Drayton, West Drayton, Dunham, Ragnall.
71 only: Flintham.

Derby Central Library.
61: Annesley 51-91; Annesley Woodhouse 51; Attenborough 51-91; Ainsworth 81; Bagthorpe 51; Basford 91; Beggar Hill 81; Beverlee 61; Blidworth 91; Blyth 51; Bramcote 51-91; Brimsley 81; Carburton 51,81,91; Carlton in Hendrick 51; Chilwell 51-91; Cossall 61-91; Cuckney 51-91; Eastwood 51,61,81; Edwinstowe 81; Fackley 81,91; Felley 51,61,81,91; Flintham 71 only; Fullwood 51,91; Gateford 51; Greasley 51-81; Haggonfield 51; Harworth 51; Hazlewood 51, 81,91; Hill Top 61,91 ; Hodsock 51; Holbeck 51-91; Holme 41,61,71,81; Hucknall 51; Hucknall Torkard 61; Kimberley 51,61,81; Kingston-upon0Soar 51-91; Kirkby 71 only; Kirkby in Ashfield 51,61,81; Mansfield 91; Mansfield Woodhouse 51; Moorgreen 51,61; Moorwood Moor 81,91; Nether Langwith 81; New Brimsley 51,61; Newthorpe 51,61; North Carlton 51; Nuthall (Nuttall) 81; Radford 51; Ratcliffe-upon- Soar 51-91; Selston 51,61; Selby 51; Shelton 91; Shireoaks 51; Skegby 51,91; South Carlton 51; Stapleford 51-91; Styyup 91; Teversall 81,91; Toton 51-91; Trent College 81; Trowell 51-91;
Watnall 61,81; Watnall Cantelupe 51,61,81; Watnall Chaworth 51,61,81; Welbeck 51; Wigthorpe 51; Worksop 51.
81: SDs of Carburton, Pleasley, Blackwell, Greasley, Ilkeston, Bulwell.

Doncaster Central Library.
51-81: Auckley, Austerfield (also 41), Blaxton, Carlton (41,81 only), Finningley, Misson, Newington (51 only). These places are probably also included in holdings at *Leeds Reference Library* and at *Wakefield M.D. Library* (both 41-81).
Note. See also *Retford Library*, above.

Nottinghamshire continued

Sheffield Archives.
N Auckley 51,71; Barlborough 41,51; Blyth 51-81;
N Carlton 51-81; S Carlton 61-81; Clowne 51;
Edwinstowe 51; Elmton 41; Goldthorpe 51-71;
Harworth 51-81; Hodsock 51-71; Holbeck 51;
Langwith 51; Loxdale 51; Misson 51-81; Norton 51;
Oldcoates 51-81; Rushbeds 51; Serlby 51,71;
Styrrup 51-81; Wallingwells 51,71; Whitwell 51;
Worksop 51.

Sheffield Central Library (Local Studies).
Blythe 81; Cuckney 71,81; Worksop 81.

OXFORDSHIRE

Census Indexes and Publications:
51: Complete transcripts for county on microfiche
and Surname Indexes (book form) published by
Oxon FHS, see *Marriage, Census & Other Indexes.*
91: Index (incl. forenames and ages) on microfiche publ. by Oxon FHS (in progress). Latest lists
and prices from Dr. H.A.Kearsey, 2 Beeching Close,
Upton, Didcot OX11 9JR.
*Church and Chapel in Oxfordshire, 1851: The
return of the census of religious worship,* ed. Kate
Tiller, Oxfordshire Record Society, **55**, 1987.

Centre for Oxon Studies, Oxford Central Library.
41-91: Oxfordshire and the former north Berkshire
(Vale of the White Horse); for former Berks.
parishes see under that county.
Note. Woodstock and Bladon 61 do not survive.
Key to places in pre-74 Oxon in 1851 census,
Oxfordshire Family Historian **2**, 3 (Autumn '80).

Oxford Brookes University Library.
51-71: Oxford city and Headington RD.

Abingdon Library.
51-91: Abingdon RD: SD of Nuneham Courtenay.

Banbury Library.
51-91: Banbury RD: SDs of Banbury, Bloxham,
Cropredy and Swalcliffe;
Brackley (Nhants.) RD: Brackley SD.

Bicester Library.
51: Bicester (town) (print-out).

Henley Library.
51-91: Henley RD: SDs of Henley, Watlington.

Witney Library.
51-91: Witney RD: SDs of Bampton, Burford,
Eynsham, Witney.

Berkshire Local Studies Library, Reading.
Caversham 41-91; Checkendon 51-91; Harpsden
41,51,81,91; Henley 41,51,91; Ipsden 51-91;
Nettlebed 51-91; Nuffield 51,61,81,91; Rotherfield
Greys 41,51,91; Rotherfield Peppard 51,91;
Shiplake 41,51,81,91.

High Wycombe Library.
51,61: Some south Oxon. parishes bordering Bucks.

Oxfordshire continued

Berkshire Record Office, Reading.
A considerable number of south Oxfordshire places
are held, mainly 51-91, too many for listing in detail
in this reprint. Full lists available at the B.R.O.

*Buckinghamshire County Reference Library
(Buckinghamshire Collection), Aylesbury)*
(duplicates at *Milton Keynes Library,* and *High
Wycombe*)
41-91: some parishes in Henley and Thame areas
bordering Buckinghamshire

Northamptonshire Record Office.
All 81, other years as shown: Banbury 71; Gt and
Lit Bourton; Clattercote; Claydon; Cropredy;
Finmere 51,71; Hanwell; Mixbury 51,71; Mollington;
Neithrop; Prescote 51; Wardington 51; Williamscott.

Warwickshire Record Office, Warwick.
81-91: Alkerton, Gt and Lit Bourton, Broughton,
Chastleton, Clattercote, Claydon, Cornwell,
Cropredy, Drayton, Enstone, Epwell, Hanwell,
Heythrop, Horley, Hornton, Mollington, Newington
North, Norton Chipping, Norton Over, Prescote (91
only), Rollright Little (81 only), Rollright Great,
Salford, Shenington, Shutford West, Sibford Ferris,
Sibford Gower, Swalcliffe, Swerford, Tadmarton,
Tew Great, Tew Little, Wroxton,
    Name index available.

RUTLAND
Now part of Leicestershire.

Census Indexes and Publications
    See *Marriage, Census and Other Indexes.*

Leicestershire Record Office, Wigston Magna.
41-81: Rutland.

Oakham Library.
51-71, 91: Rutland.
81: Part.

Peterborough Library (Cambs. C.C.).
Belmesthorpe 61-91; Gt. and Lt. Casterton
51,81,91; Clipsham 51,81,91; Essendine 51-91;
Ketton 51, 81,91; Pickworth 51, 81,91; Ryhall 51-91;
Tinwell 51,61, 81,91; Tixover 51, 81,91.
51,81: Gt and Lit Casterton, Clipsham, Ketton,
Pickworth, Tinwell, Tixover.

County Record Office, Huntingdon.
51-61,81-91: Gt and Lit Casterton; Clipsham;
Essendine 51-81; Ketton; Pickworth; Ryhall with
Belmisthorpe 51-81; Tinwell with Ingthorpe; Tixover.
Transcript: 81 (Mormon).

Northamptonshire Record Office, Northampton.
All **81**, other years as shown: Barrowden 51;
Belmisthorpe; Caldecott 71; Gt and Lit Casterton;
Clipsham; Essendine 71; Glaston; Ingthorpe;
Ketton; N and S Luffenham 71; Morcott; Pickworth;
Pilton; Ryhall 71; Seaton 51; Thorpe by Water 51;
Tinwell; Tixover 51; Toletethorpe; Wing.

SHROPSHIRE

Census Indexes and Publications:
See *Marriage, Census and Other Indexes* for
Shropshire FHS 1851 census project.

*Shropshire Records and Research Centre,
Shrewsbury.*
41-91: whole county.
Transcripts: Baschurch 51; Benthall 51; Bishop's
Castle 31,51,61; Bridgnorth (pt) 51,61; Cheswardine
81; Clee St. Margaret 41,51; Cold Weston 41;
Dawley: Hinkshay (Dawley Magna) 51; Little Dawley
51; Farlow 51; Fitz 51; Ford 51; Gt Ness 51;
Lilleshall (pt) 41,51,61,71, Little Wenlock 51; Ludlow
51; Madeley: Coalport 51; Melverley 51; Montford
51; Myddle 71,81; Newport 41,51; Selattyn 41;
Shrawardine 51; **Shrewsbury** 41-71 (part); Stanton
Lacy (pt) 41,51,61,71; Tugford 41; Wellington
21,41,51; Wem (Workhouse) 51; Wrockwardine
41,51.

Oswestry Library.
51: Oswestry and district.
81: Shropshire (Mormon index).

Staffordshire Record Office, Stafford.
71,81 unless shown otherwise: Adderley; Albrighton
(not 81); Badger; Bearstone; Beckbury; Betton (not
81); Bletchley; Boningale (Binghall); Lit Chatwell
41,71 only; Donington 61-81; Dorrington; Drayton
Magna and Parva 61,81 only; Gravenhunger;
Heaths Hill 51 only; Higford; Irelands Cross (not 81);
Kemberton 61-81; Lilleshall 61 only; Longford
61-81; Longslow (not 81); Lullington 51 only; Market
Drayton 61-81; Moreton Say; Norton; Oakengates
61,71 only; Pipe Gate (not 81); Rudge 51-71 only;
Rush Lane (not 81); Ryton; Sheriffhales 41-81;
Shifnal 61-81; Snershill (not 81); Stockton; Stretton
41 only; Styche Woodlands; Sutton Maddock; Tong
61-81; Warley 51,61,81 only; Woodseaves 61-81;
Woore.

*Hereford & Worcester Record Office, Worcester
HQ.*
51-91: Burford.
51,71,81: Boraston (not 51); Greete & 91; Nash &
91: Tilsop; Weston; Whatmore (not 81), Whitton
(not 51).

Hereford Library.
51,61: Ludlow &D.

Flintshire Record Office, Hawarden.
51-91: a few parishes bordering Denbighshire and
Flintshire.

Denbighshire Record Office, Ruthin.
41,61,91: a few parishes bordering Denbighshire.

Powys County Library, Llandrindod Wells.
51-91: Bedstone (not 71); Bettws y Crwyn;
Lit Brampton (not 81, or 91); Bucknell;
Llanfairwaterdine; Lurkenhope 51,61 only.

SOMERSET
The northern part of the county is now in the county
of Avon.

Census Indexes and Publications:
See *Marriage, Census and Other Indexes* for
Somerset & Dorset FHS and Bristol & Avon FHS
1851 index publications and search services.

Somerset Record Office, Taunton.
41-91: whole historic **county.**
81: Mormon Index.

Yeovil Library (Somerset County Council)
41: The Hundreds of, Abdick and Bulstone; Bruton;
Catsash; Crewkerne; Horethorne; Houndsborough,
Barwick and Coker; Kingsbury; Martock; Norton
Ferris; South Petherton; Pitney; Somerton; Stone;
Tintinhull.
51-91: RDs of Chard, Yeovil, Wincanton.

Bristol Central Reference Library.
41-91 unless shown otherwise: Abbots Leigh;
Backwell; Barrow Gurney; Bathampton 41;
Bedminster; Brislington; Brockley 41-81; Burnett
71,81,91; Butcombe 41,51,81,91; Cameley;
Camerton 51-91; Chelvey 41-81; Chelwood 41-91;
Chew Magna; Chew Stoke; Chewton Mendip 41,61;
Chilcompton; Clapton-in-Gordano; Claverton 41;
Cleeve 51-91; Clevedon; Clutton; Compton Dando;
Compton Martin; Corston 51-91; Dundry; Easton-in-
Gordano; Emborough 41; Failand; Farmborough;
Farrington Gurney; Felton; Flax Bourton; E and W
Harptree; High Littleton 51-91; Hinton Blewett;
Houndstreet; Kelston 51-91; Kenn 51-91;
Keynsham; Kingston Seymour 51-91; Litton 51-91;
Long Ashton; Marksbury; Midsomer Norton;
Nailsea; Nempnet; Newton St Loe 51-91;
Northstoke 51-81; Norton Malreward 51-91;
Paulton; Pensford 51-91; Pill 41,71,81,91; Portbury;
Portishead; Priston; Publow; Queen Charlton 51-91;
Radstock 51-91; Saltford 51-91; Shirehampton;
Stanton Drew; Stanton Prior 51-91; Ston 51; Ston
Easton 51-91; Stowey; Tickenham; Timsbury; Ubley
41,51,71,91; Walton-in-Gordano 41,51,71-91;
Weston-in-Gordano; Whitchurch; Wick; Wilmington
51-71; Windmill Hill 51-71; Winford; Wraxall; Yatton
51-91.
See also under Glos. and Bristol section.

Bath Central Library
41-91: Bath; Bathampton; Batheaston; Bathford;
Charlcombe (not 61); Claverton; Combe Down;
Combe Hay; Dunkerton; Englishcombe; Hinton
Charterhouse; Langridge (not 61); Monkton Combe;
St. Catherine (not 71); Southstoke (not 91);
Swainswick; Wellow; Woolley (not 61).
41: Backwell, Barrow Gurney, Batcombe, Chelvey,
Corston, Farleigh Hungerford, Forscote or Foxcote,
Kelston, Long Ashton, Newton St Loe, North Stoke,
Norton St. Philip, Tellisford, Winford.
Also Camerton 41,51; Clandon 51; Freshford
41,91; Midford 61; Peasedown 61; Radstock 51;
Shockerwick 61,81; Shoscombe 71; Stony Littleton
61; Tadwick 81; Welton 51; Woodborough 71.

Somerset continued

*Woodspring Central Library,
Weston-super-Mare.*
Most places within a 5-mile radius of Weston:
41-81: Bleadon, Hutton (not 41), Kewstoke,
Locking, Lympsham (not 41, part only 51,61), Uphill,
Weston-super-Mare, Wick St Lawrence, Worle.
61-81: Banwell, Berrow, Brean, E Brent (Edingworth
and Rooksbridge), S Brent, Burnham, Highbridge.
41 only: Loxton, Puxton, Rodney Stoke,
Rowberrow, Shipham, Winscombe.
Indexes: Family names 41-81 complete for all
census holdings, all compiled by Brian Austin.

Chard Library (Somerset C.C.).
Chard 51 (photostat).

*Frome Museum, 1 North Parade, Frome (Mrs H.M.
Massey, 8a Critchill Grove, Frome, Som BA11
4HD).*
Frome 41,51,71,81; and district 41,51,81.
Index: Frome and district 51 (16,000). pt 81.
51: Handwritten copy, Frome.

Westcountry Studies Library, Exeter.
51-91: Angersleigh; Bickenhall; Corfe; Orchard
Portman; Otterford; Pitminster; Staple Fitzpaine;
Thurlbear.
51,71-91: Brushford; Dulverton; Exmoor.
51,81-91: Exford; Exton; Hawkridge; Huish
Champflower.
51,61,81,91: Buckland St. Mary; Combe
St. Nicholas; Knowle St. Giles.
51,81: King's Brompton.

Reference Library, Dorchester, Dorset.
Buckhorn Weston 41,91; Goathill 41-91; Holwell
51-91; Kington Magna 41,91; Marston Magna
51-91; Misterton 51-91; Pointington 51,61,81;
Rimpton 51-91; Sandford Orcas 51-91; Seaborough
51-91; Trent 51-91.

Wiltshire Record Office, Trowbridge.
51-81: Freshford.

STAFFORDSHIRE
The southern tip of the county, round Walsall,
Wednesbury, West Bromwich and Wolverhampton,
is now in the county of West Midlands.

Census Indexes and Publications:
  See *Marriage, Census and Other Indexes* for
B&MSGH and other 1851 indexes.

Staffordshire Record Office, Stafford.
41-81: Whole of **Staffordshire** excl. former county
boroughs, eg Stoke-on-Trent; and parts of South
Staffs., eg parts of Walsall and Wolverhampton 61
and 71 only. A few minor omissions elsewhere
especially near county boundaries.
91: Historic county of **Staffordshire**.

Staffordshire continued

Hanley Library Information Service, Bethesda St.
41: Stoke-on-Trent area only.
51-91: Stoke-on-Trent plus **North Staffordshire**
from Stone in south to Biddulph and Knypersley in
north, excl. Newcastle area and areas around Leek
and Cheadle.
Indexes: places 41-91; Penkhull surnames 51.

Newcastle-under-Lyme Central Library.
41-91: Newcastle area.

Kidsgrove Library.
Ranscliff Township 51-71; Brieryhurst Township
51(pt),61,71 (photostats).

Burton-upon-Trent Library.
Abbots Bromley 51,61; Acton Trussell 51; Alrewas
41,61-81; Anslow 41-91; Bagots Bromley 51,61;
Barton-under-Needwood 41-91; Bednall 51;
Blithfield 51,61; Bramshall 51; Branston 41-91;
Brewood 51; Burton on Trent 41-91; Bushbury 51;
Cannock 51; Cheslyn Hay 51; Church Eaton 51;
Clifton Campville 41; Coton-in-the-Clay 41; Croxall
41; Croxden 51; Draycott-in-the-Clay 41-81;
Dunstall 41-91; Edingale 41; Elmhurst 41; Essington
51; Fauld 41; Featherstone 51; Fisherwick 41;
Fradley 41; Gratwich 51; Hamstall Ridware
41,61-81; Hanbury 41-91; Harlaston 41; Haselour
41; Hatherton 51; Haunton 41; Hednesford 51;
Hilton (nr Wolverhampton) 51; Horninglow 51-91;
Huntington 51; King's Bromley 41,61-81; Kingston
51,61; Lapley 51; Leigh 51; Marchington 41-81;
Marchington Woodlands 41-81; Mavesyn Ridware
41,61-81; Newborough 41-61; Norton Canes 51;
Oakley 41; Penkridge 51; Pipe Ridware 41,61-81;
Rolleston 41-91; Saredon 51; Shareshill 51;
Stapenhill 51-91; Streethay 41; Stretton 41-91;
Stretton (nr Penkridge) 51; Tamhorn 41; Tatenhill
41-91; Teddesley Hay 51; Thorpe Constantine 41;
Tunstall 81; Tutbury 41-91; Whittington 41; Winshill
41-91; Wolstanton 81; Wychnor 41-91; Gt Wyrley
51; Yoxall 41,61-91.
Index to individuals, Burton upon Trent 51.

Uttoxeter Library.
Abbots Bromley 41,51,71,91; Alton 41-81; Calwich
61-91; Cauldon 61-81; Croxden 41-91; Cubley
(Derbys) 51,61,81,91; Denstone 41-91; Doverodge
(Derbys) 41-91; Ellastone 41,61-91; Marchington
41-91; Mayfield 41, 61-91; Prestwood 61,71,91;
Ramshorn 61-91; Rocester 41-91; Roston (Derbys)
81,91; Snelston (Derbys) 61-91; Stanton 61,71,91;
Stramshall 91; Sudbury (Derbys) 61,81,91;
Uttoxeter 41-91; Waterfall 91; Waterhouses 61-81;
Wootton 61-91.

Lichfield Library.
41-71: Lichfield District Council area incl. parts of
neighbouring areas.
81-91: Lichfield District Council area; Tamworth and
Rugeley areas.
  Abbreviated transcript for City of Lichfield, 51, MS.
  Surname index for City of Lichfield 51-81.

Staffordshire continued

King Edward VI High School, Stafford.
Stafford area 51; Gnossall area 61.

Wolverhampton Central Library.
41-91: Present **Wolverhampton** borough and part of present South Staffordshire district, eg Codsall, Wombourne and area.

Walsall Local History Centre, Essex Street, Walsall.
41-91: South Staffs. SDs incl. all of Walsall MB. Surname index to Bloxwich part of 91 census.

West Midlands College of Higher Education, Walsall.
51-81: Borough of Walsall, SDs of Pelsall, Aldridge, Rushall, Walsall Wood and Great Barr (Aldridge).

MB of Sandwell Libraries:
Local Studies Centre, Smethwick Library
41-91 for the entire present MB of Sandwell.
Indexes: West Bromwich 51-81; Rowley Regis, Smethwick, Tipton, Wednesbury 41-81; Oldbury 41-71.

West Bromwich Library (Sandwell MB).
41-91: West Bromwich and area.

Tipton Library (Sandwell MB).
41-91: Tipton and area.
Indexes: Tipton 41-81.

Wednesbury Library (Sandwell MB).
41-91: Wednesbury and area.
Indexes: Wednesbury 41-81.

Shropshire Records and Research Centre, Shrewsbury (Local Studies Library).
41-91: Kinver, Enville, Bobbington; also places in Staffordshire near Market Drayton, Newport and Wolverhampton.

Dudley Archives and Local History Service, Coseley.
41-81: Amblecote, Brierley Hill, Coseley, Gornal (Upr and Lr), Kingswinford, Pensett, Quarry Bank, Sedgley.
41: Bobbington, Busbury, Claverley, Himley, Penn (Upr and Lr), Tettenhall.
61: Cradley Heath, Old Hill, Rowley, Tipton.
81,91: All places now in Dudley M.B.
Street indexes 51-81: Amblecote, Kingswinford, Sedgley, all places now in Dudley M.B.

Birmingham Central Library (Local Studies Div.).
41-91: all places in Staffs. now within the boundary of Birmingham, incl. or plus: Aldridge 41,61; Armitage 41; Gt Barr 41-61; Bentley 41,81; Bloxwich 41; Burntwood 41; Darlaston 41; Drayton Bassett 41; Elford 41; Farewell 41; Harborne 41-81; Handsworth 41-81; Longsdon 41; Norton-under-Cannock 41; Oscott 51,61; Pelsall 41; Rushall 41,61; Shenstone 41; Smethwick 81; Tamworth 41; Tipton 41; Walsall 41; Walsall Wood 41; Wednesbury 41,81; Wednesfield 41; West Bromwich 41,81; Willenhall 41; Wolverhampton 41-71.

Kidderminster (Worcs.) Library.
41: Amblecote, Bobbington, Codsall, Enville, Kinver, Oaken, Orton, Patshull, Pendeford, Seisdon, Wombourn.

Hereford & Worcester Record Office, Worcester HQ.
51-91: Amblecote (not 81), Kingswinford, Harborne.
51 only: Smethwick, Wordsley.

Derby Central Library (Local Studies Dept.), 25b Irongate, Derby.
Abbots Bromley 51,61; Alstonfield 51-91; Ammington and Stoneydelph 51,61,71; Anslow 51,61,81,91; Bagots Bromley 61; Barton-under-Needwood 51,61,71; Bitterscote 51, Blithfield 51,61; Blore-with-Swinscoe 51-91; Bramshall 51,61,91; Branstone 51,61,71; Brownhills 51; Burton extra 61; Burton-on-Trent 51,61; Burton on Trent Workhouse 81; Calton-in-Blore 51,61,71,91; Calton-in-Croxden 91; Calton-in-Mayfield 51,61,71,91; Calton-in-Waterfall 51,61,71,91; Calton Lees 91; Calwich 51-91; Camberford 61; Canwell 51; Church Mayfield 51; Clifton Campville 51,61; Coton 51,61; Croxall 41-71; Croxden 51-81; Croxden Abbey; Drayton Bassett 51;61; Dugdale 51,61; Dunstall 51,61; Ecton 81,91; Edingale 51,61; Ellastone 51-91; Fazeley 51,61; Gratton 41-91; Gratwich 61,91; Hales 51; Hanbury 51,61,81,91; Harlaston 51,61; Haunton 51,61; Hints 51,61; Hockley 51,91; Hopwas 51,61; Horninglow 51,61,81,91; Ilam 51-91; Kingstone 51; Leigh 51,61,91; Lightwood 51,91; Marchington 51-91; Marchington Woodlands 71-91; Mayfield 51-91; Musden Grange 51-71; Newborough 51,61; Norbet 91; Orgreave 51,71; Prestwood 51-91; Ramshorn 51-91; Rocester 51-91; Rolleston 51,61,81,91; Stafford 61; Stanshope 81,91; Stanton 41-91; Stapenhill 41-91; Stoke 41-91; Stretton 51,61,81; Swinscoe 51-91; Tamworth 51-71; Tatenhill 51,61,81,91; Thorpe Constantine 51,61; Throwley 81; Tutbury 51,61,81,91; Upper Mayfield 51; Uttoxeter 51-91; Uttoxeter Woodlands 91; Walton 61; Waterfall 51-91; Waterhouses 61,81,91; Wetton 71,81,91; Whitfield 41-91; Wichnor 51,61,81,91; Wiggington 51,61; Wilnecote 51,61; Winkhill 51-91; Winshill 41-91; Withington 91; Woodhouses 51,61,71,91; Wootton 51-91.

Derbyshire County Library, Matlock.
41-91: parishes bordering on Derbyshire including, Alstonfield, Anslow, Aston, Blore, Burton-on-Trent Workhouse, Calwich, Catton (in Blore, Mayfield, Waterfall), Coinbridge, Coton, Croxden, Croxden Abbey, Denstone, Draycott in the Clay, Ecton, Ellastone, Great Gate, Hanbury, Hope, Hopedale, Horninglow, Ilam, Mappleton, Marchington, Mayfield, Milldale, Nothill, Okeover, Prestwood, Ramshorn, Rocester, Rolleston, Stanshope, Stanton, Stretton, Swinscoe, Tatenhill, Throwley, Tutbury, Uttoxeter, Waterfall, Waterhouses, Wetton, Wichnor, Winkhill, Winshall, Wooton.

Nottingham University Library.
51-81: parishes bordering on Derbyshire.

Staffordshire continued

Warwickshire Record Office, Warwick.
Amington 41,51; Alders 91; Bolehall 41,51,81,91;
Canwell 91; Chilcote 51; Clifton Campville 91;
Coton 51,91; Croxhall 51; Comberford 51,91;
Drayton Bassett 51,81,91; Edingale 51,91; Fazeley
51,81,91; Glascote 41,51,81,91; Harlaston 51,91;
Haunton 51,91; Hints 51,81,91; Hopwas 51; Statfold
51,91; Syerscote 51,91; Thorpe Constantine 51,91;
Wigginton 51,91; Wilnecote 41,51.

Lanchester Library, Coventry.
81: Staffordshire (Mormon index).

SUFFOLK

See Suffolk Record Office *Guide to Genealogical
Sources* for full details of coverage in the three
branches; and *Marriage, Census and Other Indexes*
for Suffolk FHS 1851 index publications.

Suffolk Record Office, Ipswich.
41-71: former county of **East Suffolk.**
61: former county of **West Suffolk.**
81-91: county of **Suffolk.**
Indexes: as Lowestoft Branch.

Suffolk Record Office, Bury St Edmunds.
41: former county of **West Suffolk.**
41-71: Mutford and Lothingland Hundreds.
51: Bosmere and Claydon, Hartismere, Hoxne,
Sanford and Stow Hundreds.
51-71: former county of **West Suffolk.**
81-91: county of **Suffolk.**
Transcripts: Alpheton 41-71; Barrow 81; Beyton 51;
Groton 51; Hargrave 51; Risby 41-71; Little Wratting
51.

Suffolk Record Office, Lowestoft.
41-91: Beccles; Bungay; Halesworth; Lowestoft;
Pakefield; Southwold.
51-91: Carlton Colville; Kessingland; Kirkley;
Oulton.
61-91: Schedule of vessels.
91: Framlingham; Saxmundham; Great Yarmouth.
Indexes: 51 Lowestoft and surrounding villages;
51, 81 Beccles, 41-81 Frostenden, Schedules of
Vessels for NE Suffolk 61091 name of vessel and
personal names; 51-91: Carlton Colville,
Kessingland, Kirkley, Oulton; 91: Framlingham,
Gorleston, Ipswich, Saxmundham, Great Yarmouth.
81: arranged in sections for surname, birthplace,
place of residence on the night of the census as
enumerated and miscellaneous.

*Felixstowe FHS, c/o Margaret Lake, 16 Western
Avenue, Felixstowe, Suffolk IP11 9SB.*
51-81: Felixstowe and Walton (photocopies). Postal
enquiries, £1 + SAE.
51, 91: Woodbridge Reg. Dist. (Colneis Penninsular
and parts of Ipswich).
81: Suffolk (Mormon index).

Suffolk continued

County Record Office, Cambridge.
(**61** also at *Huntingdon Record Office*).
41: Barton Mills, Brandon, Cavenham, Santon,
Downham, Elvedon, Eriswell, Exning, Freckenham,
Herringswell, Icklingham, All Saints and St. James,
Lakenheath, Mildenhall, Tuddenham St. Mary,
Wangford, Worlington.
41,61-91: Exning, Newmarket St. Mary.
Dalham 61-91, Gazeley 61-91, Higham 61-81,
Lidgate 61091, Moulton 61-91, Ousden 61-91,
51: Indexes to Mildenhall and Risbridge districts.

Saffron Walden Library (Essex C.C.).
Acton 51; Alpheton 51; Barnardiston 51-81; Borley
41,51; Boxted 51; Cavendish 51; Clare 51-91;
Chilton 51; Clare 51-91; Glemsford 51; Gt Bradley
51-81; Hartest 51; Hawksdon 51; Hundon 51,71-91;
Lawshall 51; Liston 41,51; Melford 51; Newton 51;
Poslingford 51, 71-91; Somerton 51; Stanstead 51;
Stoke 51,71-91; Wington 81; Withersfield 51-81;
Wixoe 51, 71,91.

SURREY

See also under London (south-west) for holdings
at Lambeth, Southwark and Wandsworth covering
parishes originally in Surrey but already by 1841-
1891 forming part of the metropolis.

Census Indexes and Publications:
See *Marriage, Census and Other Indexes* for East
and West Surrey FHS published census indexes
and projects; and *Lists of Londoners* for 1851
indexes for the metropolis.

Surrey Record Office, Woking (from mid-1998).
41-71: Surrey (modern administrative county only,
excl. present Greater London area).
81: RDs of Chertsey, Guildford, Hambledon,
Dorking, Reigate, Godstone, Epsom and Farnham
(Farnham and Frimley SDs only, not Aldershot),
Staines, Croydon (Woodmansterne only), Kingston
(Esher SD only) and Windsor (Egham SD only).
91: Surrey (modern administrative county only,
excl. present Greater London area).

Guildford Branch Library (Local Studies).
41-91: Surrey (post-1974).

Ashtead Branch Library.
41-71: Ashtead parish (photostats).

Chertsey Library.
51,71: Chertsey parish (Addlestone, New Haw,
Woodham, Ottershaw, Lyne, Longcross).

Croydon Local Studies Library.
41-91: Croydon.
Index to people 51; to streets 41-91.
See also *Bromley (Kent) Central Library,* right.

Dorking Branch Library.
41-71: Dorking parish (photostats).

Surrey continued

Esher Branch Library.
41-61: Esher, Cobham, Molesey, Dittons (area of old Esher UDC) (photocopies).

Ewell Library.
41-71: Epsom and Ewell (photocopies).
81-91: Epsom and Ewell (microform).

Kingston-upon-Thames Heritage Centre.
Chessington 41; Cuddington 41-71; Epsom and Ewell 41-71; Ham 41-71; Hook 41-71; Kingston All SS 41-71; Kingston St. Peter 51-71; Kingston Vale 51-71; Old Malden 71; New Malden 61,71; Richmond 41; Surbiton 41; (St. Mark) 51-71; (Christchurch) 71; Thames/Long Ditton 41; Wimbledon (incomplete) 41,51.
81: RDs of Kingston-upon-Thames, Malden, Esher (incl. Thames Ditton and pt of Long Ditton), and Hampton (incl. Hampton Wick and Teddington).
91: Epsom; Chessington; Cuddington; Kingston; Ham; Hook; Malden; Wimbledon.

Leatherhead Branch Library.
41-71: Bookham, Fetcham (51,61 missing), Leatherhead, civil parishes (photocopies).

Mitcham Library (LB of Merton).
41-71: Mitcham (full size copy).
Name index to Mitcham parish 41,51,61;
91: Mitcham, Morden; Merton and Wimbledon.

Morden Library (LB of Merton).
41-71: Merton and Morden (full size).
Name indexes: 41,51.
81-91: Merton, Morden, Mitcham and Wimbledon.

Richmond Local Studies Library.
41,51: Richmond parliamentary constituency covering Richmond, Kew, Petersham, Ham, Barnes and Mortlake (photocopy).
61-91: area covered by the LB of Richmond on Thames.

Sutton Central Library.
41-91: Beddington (61 mainly lost), Carshalton, Cheam, Sutton, Wallington (present LB of Sutton);
61-91: Woodmansterne; South Metropolitan District Schools (in Sutton).
51-91: Banstead.
41,81,91: Mitcham; Morden.
01,01: Merton; Warehousemen & Clerks' School, Russell Hill, Beddington; Holborn Union Industrial Schools, Mitcham; Middlesex County Lunatic Asylum, Banstead.
91: Holburn Union Workhouse, Mitcham; Female Orphan Asylum, Beddington.
Surname Indexes to 41-81 census; street index to 81 census (LBS area only).

Wimbledon Reference Library (LB of Merton).
41-91: Merton, Mitcham, Morden, Wimbledon (mf); also Wimbledon (full size copy).
51: Name index to Wimbledon parish.
81: Street index to Wimbledon parish.
See also *Mitcham* and *Morden Libraries.*

Uxbridge Library (LB of Hillingdon).
51, 71-91: Staines (part).

Bromley (Kent) Central Library.
Addington 51; Barnes 41; Battersea 41; Coulsdon 51,71(pt); Croydon 51-71; Norwood 81; Penge 41-81; Sanderstead 51.

East Sussex Record Office, Lewes.
Felbridge 81,91; Lingfield 51,61,81,91.

Berkshire Record Office, Reading.
Egham 51-91; Thorpe 61-91.

SUSSEX

Census Indexes and Publications:
See *Marriage, Census and Other Indexes* for East and West Sussex 1851 Census Index publications, Brighton 1841 index and other projects.
The Religious Census of Sussex, 1851, ed. A. Vickers, Sussex Record Society, 1989.

Brighton Central Reference Library.
41-91: whole county of Sussex.
In-house street index to Brighton, 41.
Billenness: partial index, 51; extracts from 41,61.

Hastings Central Library (Local Studies), Brassey Institute.
41: Hastings area (SDs of Baldslow, Battle, Bexhill, Burwash, Etchingham, Foxearle, Goldspur, Gostrow, Guestling, Hastings, Hawkhurst, Heathfield, Netherfield, Ninfield, Staple).
51-91: whole county of Sussex (E and W).

East Sussex Record Office, Lewes.
41: All post-1974 **East Sussex** and (in post-1974 West Sussex): Edburton, E Grinstead, Horsted Keynes, Lindfield, Newtimber, Poynings, Pyecombe.
51: All pre-1974 **East Sussex** and (in pre-1974 West Sussex): Botolphs, Coombes, Cowfold, Kingston Buci, New and Old Shoreham, Sompting, Southwick.
61: All pre-1974 **East Sussex** (incl. Brighton plus Brighton street index) and pre-1974 West Sussex places as for 51.
71: All post-1974 **East Sussex.**
81: All pre-1974 **East Sussex** and pre-1974 West Sussex places as for 51 + Lancing.
91: All pre-1974 **East Sussex** and pre-1974 West Sussex places as for 51 + Lancing.
Transcripts (asterisked places indexed):
Chalvington 61; Chiddingly 41,51; Folkington 41,51; Frant 51*; Glynde 41*-81*; Hansey 51,81; Hartfield 51*; Heathfield 71*; Herstmonceux 41,51,71; E Hoathly 51; Laughton 51; Ringmer 41*-81*; Rotherfield 51*; Waldron 71*; Warbleton 41,51*; Wartling 41,51,71; Withyham 51.

Sussex continued

Eastbourne Library.
41-81: Eastbourne, Hailsham, Hellingly, Westham.
91: East and West Sussex.

Hove Area Library.
41-91: Hove, Brighton.
Street index to Hove 51-81.

Worthing Library (West Sussex C.C.)
41-91: County of **West Sussex** (post-1974).

Bognor Regis, Burgess Hill, Crawley, East Grinstead, Haywards Heath, Horsham, Littlehampton and Shoreham-by-the-Sea Libraries:
41-91: own catchment areas only

West Sussex Record Office, Chichester.
41-81: County of **West Sussex** (post 1974, incl former East Sussex parishes transferred in 1974).
91: Counties of **West** and **East Sussex**.
Indexes: Handlist, constantly updated, available of surname indexes to many individual parishes.

West Sussex Institute of Higher Education, Bognor Regis College.
41: S Bersted, E Lavant, Pagham, Madehurst, Middleton.
51: Arundel, Chichester and intervening district.
61: Brighton (Kemptown, St. Peter's, Palace); Hove, Shoreham and district. Much of West Sussex, but excl. city of Chichester.

Tunbridge Wells (Kent) Library.
41-91: Brenchley, Cranbrook, Hawkhurst, Pembury
81: Bells Yew Green 71,81; Eridge 41,71,81; Frant
51,71,81: Groomsbridge 61-81(pt).

Surrey Record Office,Woking (from mid-1998).
51: Crawley, E.Grinstead, Hartfield, W Hoathly, Withyham, Worth.
61: E. Grinstead.

WARWICKSHIRE
The north-west, Birmingham and Coventry area, is now in the county of West Midlands.

Census Indexes and Publications:
 See *Marriage, Census and Other Indexes* for B&MSGH 1851 census index microfiches and search service.
 See *Tracing Your Ancestry in Warwickshire*, June Watkins and Pauline Saul, B&MSGH, 1996, for exact location all 41-81 census mf for all Warw. parishes.

Warwickshire Record Office, Warwick.
41-91: whole county (pre-1974) (excl. Birmingham and some parishes on county boundaries).

Birmingham Central Library (Local Studies).
41-91: all districts within boundary of Birmingham, incl. Sutton Coldfield, and a wide area round Birmingham, principally 51-91.

Warwickshire continued

City of Coventry, City Record Office.
41, 51: Coventry City.

Coventry Central Library (Local Studies Collection).
Allesley 41-91; Anstey 41-91; Ashow 91; Baginton 41,91; Bedworth 51-91; Berkswell 91; Binley 51-91; Bubbenhall 91; Corley 71,91; Coundon 41-91; Coventry 41-91; Exhall (nr.Coventry) 41-91; Fillongley 71,91; Foleshill 41-91; Great Packington 71,91; Hampton-in-Arden 71,91; Honiley 91; Kenilworth 91; Keresley 41-91; Kinwalsey 71,91; Leek Wootton 91; Little Packington 71,91; Meriden 71,91; Shilton 51-91; Sowe 41-91; Stivichall 41-91; Stoke 41-91; Stoneleigh 91; Willenhall 41-91; Withybrook 51-91; Wolvey 51; Wyken 41-91.

Lanchester Library, Much Park St, Coventry.
81: Warwickshire (Mormon index).

Warwickshire County Library:
Libraries at *Leamington, Nuneaton, Rugby* and *Stratford-upon-Avon* have **41-91** for own areas.
Libraries at *Atherstone, Bedworth, Kenilworth* and *Warwick* have **91** only, for own areas, with possibility of acquiring 41-81 in due course.

Shakespeare Birthplace Trust Records Office, Stratford-upon-Avon.
41: Arrow, Oversley, Aston Cantlow, Bidford, Billesley, Binton, Exhall, Haselor, Salford Priors, Old Stratford, Luddington, Stratford-upon-Avon Borough, Temple Grafton, Welford-on-Avon.
51: Old Stratford, Stratford-upon-Avon.
61: Stratford-upon-Avon Borough, Snitterfield, Clifford Chambers, Atherstone-on-Stour, Preston-on-Stour, Alderminster, Whitchurch, Alveston, Dorsington, Welford-on-Avon, Weston-on-Avon, Long Marston, Binton, Billesley, Temple Grafton.
71: Old Stratford, Stratford-upon-Avon Borough.
81: Old Stratford; Stratford-upon-Avon Borough, Snitterfield, Clifford Chambers, Atherstone-on-Stour, Preston-on-Stour, Alderminster, Whitchurch, Alveston, Dorsington, Welford-on-Avon, Weston-on-Avon, Long Marston, Binton, Billesley, Temple Grafton, Old Stratford, Luddington.
91: Old Stratford, Stratford-upon-Avon Borough, Alveston, Charlecote, Compton Verney, Combrook, Ettington, Hampton Lucy, Kineton, Loxley, Moreton Morrell, Newbold Pacey, Wellesbourne, Luddington, Clifford Chambers, Atherstone-on-Stour, Preston-on-Stour, Alderminster, Whitchurch, Dorsington, Welford-on-Avon, Long Marston, Weston-on-Avon, Binton, Billesley, Temple Grafton, Bearley, Langley, Wolverton, Claverdon, Preston Bagot, Beaudesert, Wootton Wawen, Henley-in-Arden, Ullenhall, Snitterfield.

Solihull Central Library (Local Studies).
41-91: Solihull and all places within the MB of Solihull.

Banbury (Oxon.) Library.
51-81: as Oxford.
91: local area only (as for 51-81).

Warwickshire continued

Centre for Oxon Studies, Oxford Central Library.
51-81: Avon Dassett (not 71), Barton-on-the-Heath, Lit and Long Compton, Farnborough, Radway, Ratley, Shotteswell, Warmington.
91: Warwickshire.

Northamptonshire Record Office.
81: Arlescote, Avon Dassett, Biggin, Clifton on Dunsmore, Copson, Farnborough, Hillmorton (also 51), Mollington, Monks Kirby, Newbold Revel, Newnham Paddox, Newton, Pailton, Shotteswell, Stretton under Fosse, Willey.

Leicestershire Record Office.
41-91: parishes bordering on Leics.

Derby Central Library (Local Studies), Matlock.
Amington 51,61,71; Austrey 51,71; Boleshall and Glascote 51,61; Castle Liberty 51,61; Cliff 51,61; Holt 61; Hurley 61; Kingsbury 51,61; Middleton 51,61; Newton Regis 51,61,71, Nomans Heath 51,61,71; Seckington 51,61,71; Shuttington 51,71; Stoneydelph 51,61,71; Whateley 61.

Staffordshire Record Office, Stafford.
Austrey 51-81; Bolehill with Glascote 51-81; Bodymoor Heath 71; Cliff 51; Holloughton 51; Hurley 71; Kingsbury 51-81; Middleton 51-81; Newton Regis (Kings Newton) 51-81; Nomans Heath 51-71; Seckington 51-81; Shuttington 51-81.

Hereford & Worcester Record Office, Worcester HQ.
41 only: Alderminster, Newbold-on-Stour, Oldberrow, Shipston-on-Stour, Tidmington, Tredington, Yardley.
51 only: Quinton.
41-91: Edgbaston (not 41), Harborne (not 41), Kings Norton, Northfield.

Gloucestershire Record Office, Gloucester.
51: Barcheston, Brailes, Burmington, Butlers Marston, Cherrington, Compton Wynyates, Halford, Honington, Idlicote, Ilmington, Oxhill, Pillerton Hersey and Priors, Shipston on Stour, Stretton on the Fosse, Tidmington, Tredington, Tysoe, Whatcote, Whichford, Gt and Lit Wolford.

Gloucester Library.
41-81: parishes bordering Gloucestershire.

WESTMORLAND
Now part of Cumbria.

Census Indexes and Publications:
See *Marriage, Census and Other Indexes* for Cumbria FHS 1851 published indexes and other census projects.

Kendal Library (Cumbria County Council).
41-91: Westmorland.

Cumbria Record Office, Kendal.
Ambleside 51; Applethwaite 51; Arnside 41; Asby 51; Askham 51; Bampton 51; Barbon 41,51; Barton 51; Beetham 51,81; Birkbeck Fells 51; Bretherdale 51; Brigsteer 51; Brougham 51; Burton (Warcop) 51; Burton-in-Kendal 51,81; Casterton 51,81; Crook 51; Crosthwaite-cum-Lyth 51; Dillicar 51; Docker 51; Farleton 51; Fawcett Forest 51; Firbank 41,51; Grasmere 51,81; Grayrigg 51; Haverbrack 51; Hay and Hutton in the Hay 51,81; Helsington 51; Heversham 51; Hincaster 51; Holme 51,81; Hugill 51,81; Hutton Roof 41,51,81; Kendal 51,81; Kentmere 51,81; Killington 41,51; Kings Meaburn 81; Kirkby Lonsdale 51,81; Lambrigg 51,81; Langdale (Orton) 51,81; Langdales 51,81; Levens 51; Longsleddale 51; Lowther 51; Lupton 41,51; Mansergh 41,51; Martindale 51; Meathop & Ulpha 51; Middleton 41,51,81; Milnthorpe 51; Natland 41,51; Nether Staveley 51,81; New Hutton 51; Newbiggin 81; Old Hutton & Holmescales 51; Orton 51; Over Staveley 51,81; Patterdale 51; Patton 51; Preston Patrick 51; Raisbeck 51; Ravenstone 51,81; Rydal & Loughrigg 51,81; Sandford 51; Scalthwaiterigg 51; Sedgwick 51; Selside 51,81; Skelsmergh 51,81; Sockbridge and Tirril 51; Stainton 51; Storth 41; Strickland Ketel 51,81; Strickland Roger 51,81; Stramongate (in Kendal) 51; Tebay 41,51,71,81; Troutbeck 51,81; Underbarrow and Bradleyfield 51; Undermilbeck 51,81; Warcop 51; Whinfell 51,81; Whitwell 51,81; Witherslack 51,61,71,81; Yanwath and Eamont Bridge 51.

WILTSHIRE

Census Indexes:
See *Marriage, Census and Other Indexes* for 1851 computerised census indexes (The Nimrod Index and Wiltshire FHS).

Wiltshire Record Office, Trowbridge.
41-91: Whole county. Many of these reels belong to Wiltshire Library and Museum Service, but are kept for consultation in the Wiltshire Record Office.

Wiltshire Library and Museum Service.
41-91: Whole county. This second set, covering the whole county, is kept for lending to certain Wiltshire libraries *(Chippenham, Devizes, Marlborough, Salisbury, Swindon, Trowbridge, Warminster)* to satisfy requests. These reels are not loaned outside Wiltshire. In addition, *Salisbury* and *Swindon* hold their own copies of returns for their areas (see below). Full details are provided in a booklet, *Wiltshire Census Returns 1841-1891*, 4th ed., 1994, available from the Local Studies Officer, Wiltshire Library and Museum Service, Bythesea Road, Trowbridge, Wilts BA14 8BS.

Salisbury Library.
41-91: parishes in Salisbury area.

Swindon Library.
41-91: parishes in Swindon area.

Dorchester Reference Library, Dorset.
41-91: whole county (pre 1974).

Oxford Central Library (Local Studies).
91: whole county.
Inglesham 41; Knighton Compton 51; Oxenwood 41; Shalbourne 41.

Berkshire Record Office, Reading.
Aldbourne 51-91; Baydon 51-91; Buttermere 51,71-91; Chilton Foliatt 41-91; Froxfield 51-91; Great Bedwyn 51-91; Ham 51-91; Chisbury 51,91; Crofton 51,91; East Grafton 51,91; Hippenscombe 51,71,91; Lit Bedwyn 51,91; Marten 51,91; Ramsbury 51-91; Shalbourne 41-91; Tidcombe 51,71-91; West Grafton 51,91; Wexcombe 91; Wilton 51.

Somerset Record Office, Taunton.
41 only: Maiden Bradley, Stourton.

WORCESTERSHIRE
Now part of Hereford & Worcester, northern tip in the county of West Midlands.

Census Indexes and Publications:
See *Marriage, Census and Other Indexes* for B&MSGH 1851 index publications.

Hereford & Worcester Record Office, County Hall, Spetchley Road, Worcester.
41-91: whole of former county of **Worcestershire** (except a few omissions mostly on borders of county, eg, Inkberrow 61-81; Wythall 41,71-81; Dudley 81).
Transcripts, 51: Shrawley; Worcester St. Martin's.

Worcestershire continued

Details of holdings in libraries at Birmingham Reference (Local Studies) (B), Dudley (D), Kidderminster (K), Redditch (R) and Sandwell MB: Smethwick (S) (see note under Staffordshire).

4 = 1841; 5 = 1851; 6 = 1861; 7 = 1871; 8 = 1881; 9 = 1891. Probably more 1891 than shown.

Alvechurch R5-8,D5,B6; Upr Arley K678; Armscott K4; Belbroughton K4,B46,D56; Upr and Lr Bentley K4; Bentley Pauncefoot D45,B46,R5-8; Beoley R57,B6789; Bewdley K6-8; Bickenhill B9; Blackheath B9; Blackwell K4; Blakedown K4; Bromsgrove B46,D5,R8; Broome K468; Cakemore D4-7,B8; Catshill B4,D5; Chaddesley Corbett K4-8,B4; Churchill K468,B4; Church Lench B4,D4,K4; Clent K4,D56,B6; Cobley R5-8,D5; Cofton Hackett B46,K4,D5,R5-8; Coleshill B9; Coughton R5; Cradley D4-7,B46,K4; Dillingscott K4; Dodderhill B4,K4; Doddington K4; Doverdale B4; Dowles K7; Droitwich K4; Dudley D4-7,B6; Elmbridge K4; Elmdon B9; Elmley Lovell B4,D4,K4; Feckenham D4,K4,B45,R58; Franche B4,K7; Frankley K4,D45,B46; Grafton Manor D4,K4; Habberley B4; Hadzor B4,D4; Hagley D567,B46,K4; Halesowen D4-7,B69; Upr and Lr Halfshire K4; Hampton Lovatt B4,D4,K4; Hartlebury B4,D4; Hasbury D4-7; Hawne D4-7; Hill D4-7,B8; Hillhampton K4; Hollymoor B45; Hollywood B45; Hoobrook K5; Hunnington B6,D6; Hurcott B4,K4; Illey D4-7,B6; Inkberrow B58; Inkford B457; Ipsley B5,R58; Katchems End K5; Kidderminster K4-8,B4,D4; Kings Norton B4-8,D4,K4; Kington B4,K4; Lapal D4-7, B56; Lea Marston B9; Lutley D4-7,B4,K4; Lye and Wollescote D4-7; Mamble K4; Martley K4; Maxstoke B9; Lr Mitton (Stourport) K4-8,B4; Upr Mitton B4,K4; Morton Bagot R8; Nether Whitacre B9; Newbold K4; Northfield B4-8,D4,K4; Oldberrow R8; Oldbury (Langley) D4; Oldbury (Warley) S4-8,D4,B6-8; Oldswinford D4-7,B4,K4; Olton B9; Oswaldslow K4; Over Whitacre B9; Patingham K4; Pedmore D456,B46,K4; Redditch B46,K4,R5-8,D45; Rednall B47; Ribbesford (Bewdley) K4; Ridgeacre D4-7,B8; Rock K4; Romsley D56,B6; Rubery B4-7; Rushock K4-8,B4,D4; Salwarpe B4,D4,K4; Sambourne R58; Sedgeberrow K4; Shenstone B4; Shipston-on-Stour K4; Shirley B9; Shustoke B9; Smethwick S4-8,B4-9; Solihull B9; Spernall R8; Spetchley K4; Stoke Prior K4,D5,B6; Stone K4-8,B4; Stoulton K4; Stourbridge D4-7,B46,K4; Stourport K7; Studley R58; Tardebigge D4,K4,R5,B6; Tibberton K4; Trimpley B4; Tutnall R5-8,D5; Upton Warren B4,D4,K4; Warley B4-8,S4-8,D4,K4; Warley Wigorn D41; Warndon K4; Webheath K45,B46,R5-8; Welland K4; Westwood Park D4; Wichenford K4; Wollaston (Stourbridge) D4-7; Wolverley K4678; Woodhouse B4,K4; Wribbenall B4,K567; Wythall B4-9; Yardley D4,K4,B8; Yardley Wood B8.

Indexes: Name: Oldbury 41-71 (Smethwick Lib.); Street: Dudley (MBC) 41-81, Stourbridge 51.

Worcestershire continued

Shropshire Records and Research Centre, Shrewsbury (Local Studies Library).
91: Tenbury RD; also ?41-91, places in Worcestershire nr Kidderminster.

Hereford Library.
61: Tenbury.

Gloucestershire Record Office.
51: Broad Marston, Church Honeybourne, Pebworth, Sedgeberrow, Wickhamford.

Warwickshire Record Office, Warwick.
Acocks Green 91; Abbots Morton 51,61,81,91; Aston Magna 91; Blockley 51-91; Feckenham 51-91; Inkberrow 51-91; Ipsley 41-81; Shipston-on-Stour 51-81; Sparkhill 91; Tutnal Cum Cobley (Tardebigg) 41; Wythall 91; Yardley 51-91.

Staffordshire Record Office, Stafford.
Amblecote 41,51,71,81; Bewdley 81; Broom 41,51; Clent 41,51; Halesowen 51; Holloway 61; Holy Cross 51; Oldbury 51,61,81; Old Swinford 71; Ribbesford 81; Stourbridge 71; Warley 51,61,81.

University College of Wales, Aberystwyth.
51,71: Worcester (city).

YORKSHIRE: EAST RIDING
Now mainly in Humberside; north and west borders in North Yorkshire.

Census Indexes and Publications:
See *Marriage, Census and Other Indexes* for East Yorkshire FHS and Cleveland FHS1851 census projects and publications.

Leeds Central Local & Family History Library.
41-91: East Riding complete.
Place index.

Beverley Local Studies Library.
41-81: All **East Riding** (incomplete coverage for Hull).
91: East Riding complete, including Hull.

Humberside Archive Service, Beverley.
41-71: All **East Riding** except Hull Holy Trinity and St. Mary.
81,91: East Riding complete.
Place Indexes. street indexes to Deverley, Bridlington, Great Driffield, Hedon, Hessle, Hornsea, Hull, Pocklington, Sculcoates, Withernsea.

Hull Central Library.
41,61-91: Hull and Sculcoates RDs (ie Hull and immediate area).
51: East Riding complete, incl. Hull and Sculcoates RDs.
Street indexes: Hull and Sculcoates 41-81; Beverley 51; indexes by village, for East Riding, etc, 51.

Doncaster Central Library.
Hessle 41,81.

YORKSHIRE: NORTH RIDING and YORK
Now mainly in North Yorkshire, with northern borders in Co. Durham and Cleveland.

Census Indexes and Publications:
See *Marriage, Census and Other Indexes* for Cleveland FHS 1851 census project and publications; also North Yorkshire RO publications.

Leeds Central Local & Family History Library.
41-91: North Riding complete; Place index.

North Yorkshire County Record Office, Northallerton.
51: county of **North Yorkshire**, part of the southern part of Cleveland and some bordering areas, incl. Hemsworth, Pontefract.

Cleveland Archives Dept., Exchange House, 6 Marton Road, Middlesbrough.
41-91: part of **North Riding** now in Cleveland (incl. Middlesbrough, Thornaby, Yarm, Eston, Redcar and Guisborough).

Middlesbrough Central Library.
41-91: Middlesbrough plus those parts of the old North Riding now in Cleveland.
Name index 51· (Cleveland FHS).

Redcar District Library.
41-91: Redcar area.
Name index 51 (Cleveland FHS).

Teesside Polytechnic Library, Flatts Lane Centre, Normanby, Middlesbrough.
51 (also 61,71 if shown): Acklam 61; Ainthorpe 61 only; Aislaby; Brotton 71; Carlton; Castleton 61 only; Castlevington; Commondale 61; Danby 61; Easington; Egglescliffe; Eston; Grinton; Guisborough 61; Hartburn; Hilton; Hutton Lowcross 61; Ingleby Barwick; Kirkleatham; Kirkleavington 61; Linthorpe 61; Liverton; Loftus; Longnewton; Maltby; Marske; Middlesbrough; Moorsholm; Morton 61; Newsham; Newton 61; Normanby; Norton; Ormesby; Pickton 61; Pinchingthorpe 61; Preston; Redcar 71 (south side); Redmarshall; Skelton 71; Skinningrove; Stainton 61; Stanghaw 71; Stockton; Thornaby; Tockets; Upleatham 71; Upsall 61; Westerdale 61; Whitton; Wilton; High Worsall 61; Low Worsall; Yarm 61.

Northallerton Library.
41-91: Hambleton and Richmondshire RDs.

Scarborough Central Library.
41: Wapentakes of Dickering, Buckrose, Birdforth, Bulmer, Pickering Lythe, Ryedale, Scarborough, Langbaurgh East, Whitby Strand.
51-91: RDs of Scarborough, Driffield, Bridlington, Malton, Helmsley, Kirkby Moorside, Pickering, Whitby.
Photocopy: Falsgrave township 51.
Street index: Scarborough 41-91.

Skipton Library.
41-91: Craven District including Skipton and Settle.

Yorkshire: North Riding continued

Harrogate Central Library.
41-91: Harrogate District which includes Bilton with Harrogate, Pannal, Ripon, Pateley Bridge, Knaresborough and Boroughbridge.
51: Surname index in progress.

York Central Library.
41: York City and Ainsty. Easingwold area.
51-91: present York and Selby districts plus some bordering places. Easingwold area.

Beverley Local Studies Library.
61,81 only: York (51 complete, 81 in part); Malton, Scarborough and some other North Riding parishes in those RDs.

Hull Central Library.
51: Scarborough and Malton RDs.

Humberside Archive Service, Beverley.
91: Osbaldwick, Heworth, Murton, Stockton on the Forest, Warthill, Holtby, Gate Helmsley, Upper Helmsley, Strensall, Lillings Ambo, Flaxton, Harton, Claxton, Sand Hutton, Buttercrambe, Bossall, Gristhorpe, Lebberston, Cayton.

Durham County Record Office (**R**) and *Darlington Library* (**L**).
4 = 41; 5 = 51; 6 = 61; 7 = 71; 8 = 81 9 = 91.
Acklam L4,R5-79; Aldrough L7; W Appleton L7; Barforth L4-9,R5-9; Barningham L4-9,R5-9; Barton L4-9,R5-9; Boldron L4-9,R5-9; Bolton-on-Swale L47; Bowes L4-9,R5-9; Brignall L4-9,R5-9; Caldwell L47; Carkin L47; Castle Leavington L4,R56; Catterick L7; Cleasby L4-9,R5-9; Cliffe L4-9, R5-9; Colburn L7; Cotherstone L4-9,R5-9; Craike L4,R4-7,9; Croft L4-9,R5-9; Dalton-on-Tees R5679; Durham City (Castle Precincts) L9; Durham City (College) L9; Eggleston Abbey L4-9,R5-9; Ellerton-on-Swale L47; Eppleby L7; Eryholme L4-9,R5-9; Forcett L7; Gayles L47; Gilling L478; Gilmonby L4-9,R5-9; Girsby L5-9,R678; Greta Bridge L9,R6-8; Halnaby LR7; High Worsall R5-7,9; Holwick L4-9,R5-9; Hope L5-9,R5-9; Hunderthwaite L4-9,R5-9; Hutton Magna L4-68,R5-9; Ingleby Barwick L4,R5-7,9; Kirby Hill L47; Kirk Levington L4,R5-7,9; Lartington L4-9,R578; E and W Layton L47; Linthorpe L4,R57; Lune R578; Lunedale L4-9; Maltby L4,R57; Manfield L4-9,R578; Mickleton L4-9; Middleton R57; Middlesbrough R57; Monkend L7; Moulton L7; New Forest L47; Newsham L47; Newton Morrell L4-9,R578; Over Dinsdale L5-9,R578; Ovington L4-9,578; Picton L4,R57; Ravensworth L47; Rokeby L4-9,R578; Romaldkirk L4-9,R578; Scargill L4-9,R578; Scorton L47; Scotton L7; Smeaton R7; Sockburn L4-9; Stainton L4-9,R578; Stanwick St John L478; Stapleton L4-9,R578; Startforth L4-9,R578; Thornaby L4,R57; Thornton R7; Thorpe L46-8,R78; Tunstall L9; Uckerby L4; Warsall R7; Westwick L4-9; Whashton L47; Whorlton L4-9; Wycliffe L5-9,R78; Yarm L4,R5. (Many more places listed, too many to show here).

Wigan Archives (Lancs).
Leyburn area. **61,71:** Arrathorne, Barden, Bellerby, Constable Burton, Finghall, Garriston, Harmby, E and W Hauxwell, Hornby, Hunton, Hutton Hang, Newton le Willows, Patrick Brompton.
61 only: Burton-upon-Yore.
71 only: Akebar, Castle Bolton, Leyburn, Preston, Redmire, Spennithorne, Thornton Steward, Wensley.

Clitheroe (Lancs) Library.
41: Austwick, Bentham, Burton-in-Lonsdale, Clapham-with-Newby, Dent, Garsdale, Giggleswick, Halton Gill, Hawkswick, Horton-in-Ribblesdale, Langcliffe, Lawkland, Litton, Nappa, Rathmell, Sedbergh, Settle, Stainforth, Swinden, Thornton-in-Lonsdale.
91: Alston, Balderstone, Barrow, Bashall Eaves, Billington, Bolton by Bowland, Bowland Forest (Higher and Lower Divs), Chaigley, Chatburn, Chipping, Clayton-le-Dale, Clitheroe, Dilworth, Dinckley, Downham, Dutton, Easington, Gisburn, Gisburn Forest, Goldshaw Booth, Grindleton, Heyhouses, Horton, Hurst Green, Knowle Green, Langho, Little Bowland, Leagram, Mearley, Mellor, Middop, Mitton, Newsholme, Newton, Osbaldeston, Paythorne, Pendleton, Ramsgreave, Read, Ribchester, Rimington, Sabden, Salesbury, Sawley, Simonstone, Slaidburn, Stonyhurst College, Thornley with Wheatley, Tosside, Twiston, Waddington, West Bradford, Whalley, Wilpshire, Wiswell, Worston.

Nelson (Lancs.) Library.
Bank Newton 41,51,81; Barden 41,81; Farnhill 51,81; Hawkswick 41,81.

YORKSHIRE: WEST RIDING

Now split between West, South and North Yorkshire, with western border areas in Cumbria, Lancashire and Greater Manchester; eastern Goole area in Humberside.

Census Indexes and Publications:
See *Marriage, Census and Other Indexes* for FHS census index projects, mainly 1851.

Note. See also under Yorkshire: North Riding, above, for places formerly in the West Riding but now in the county of North Yorkshire.

WEST YORKSHIRE (post-1974)

Wakefield Library HQ, Wakefield.
41-81: West Riding complete (set owned by Yorks. and Humberside Joint Services, available to libraries in the region).
41-91: Wakefield Metropolitan District. Wakefield 61, transcript in progress. Wakefield 71: transcript, list of streets (part only).
Ossett 71, transcript, part only; Normanton 71, transcript (part only); Stanley cum Wrenthorpe 71, transcript (part only); Warmfield 71, transcript; Emley 71, transcript (part only); Flockton 71, transcript; Middlestown 71, transcript (part only).

Castleford Library (Wakefield M.D.)
81: Castleford, Whitwood, Glasshoughton.
91: Normanton, Altofts, Newland, Stanley cum Wrenthorpe, Knottingley, Fairburn Byram with Poole, Burton Salmon, Ferry Fryston, Ferrybridge, Holmfield, Wheldale, Water Fryston, Brotherton, Ackton, Loscoe Grove, Snydale, Whitwood, Glasshoughton, Castleford, Oulton with Woodlesford, Rothwell, Aberford, Allerton Bywater, Barwick in Elmet, Garforth, Kippax, Ledsham, Ledston, Swillington, Micklefield, Lotherton cum Aberford, Great and Little Preston.

Pontefract Library (Wakefield M.D.).
41-71: Carleton, N and S Elmsall, Foulby, E and W Hardwick, Hessle, Hilltop, Kirk Smeaton, S Kirkby, Knottingley, Monkhill, Nostell, Owston, Park district, Pontefract, Skellow, Tansheld.
81: Pontefract, Acton, Knottingley, Stapleton, Womersley.
91: Knottingley, Brotherton, Hillam, Beal, Ferrybridge, Fryston, Cridling Stubbs, Kellingley, Monk Fryston, Burton Salmon, Bryam cum Sutton, Fairburn, Birkin, Ackton, Streethouse, Snydale, Carleton, East Hardswick, Darrington, Featherstone, Purston Jaglin, Pontefract, Whitwood, Glasshoughton, Methley, Castleford, Ackworth Brierly, Hessle and Hill Top, West Hardwicke, Huntwick with Nostell and Foulby, Wintersett, Ryhill, Havercroft with Cold Hiendley, South Hiendley, Shafton, Hemsworth, Badsworth, Upton, Thorpe Audlin, Kirk Smeaton, Little Smeaton, Stubbs, Walden, Skelbrooke, Hamphall Stubbs, North Elmsall, Minsthorpe, Wrangbrooke, South Elmsall, South Kirkby, Great Houghton, Little Houghton.

Ossett Library.
91: Ossett with Gawthorpe, West Bretton, Emley, Flockton, Shitlington, Midgley.

Horbury and Hemsworth Libraries.
91: both hold census for own areas.

Leeds Local & Family History Library.
41-91: West Riding complete.
Street indexes, Leeds 41,51,61,81,91 (PRO); 71 (own index); district index to Leeds and immediate area 41-81; place index for all West Riding.
A series of personal name indexes to the 1851 census, published by the Yorkshire Archaeological Society, covers the old Leeds Township and many of its suburbs.

Bradford Central (Reference) Library.
Bradford (pre-74 county borough) **41-91:** Baildon; Bingley; Calverley; Denholm; Pudsey; Queensbury (part); Shipley, Wilsden.
91: Addingham; Askwith; Barden; Beamsley; Bolton Abbey; Bradleys Both; Denton; Draughton; Drighlington; Farnhill; Hazelwood with Storiths; keighley; Kildwick; Nesfield with Langbar; Shelf; Silsden; Steeton with Eastburn; Weston.
Various: Bramhope 41; Burley 41,91; Cleckheaton 51-91; Guiseley 51,71,81; Harthead-cum-Clitton 41; Hawksworth 41,51,81; Haworth 51,91; Heckmondwike 41; Hunsworth 41,51,81; Ilkley 41,91; Liversedge 41; Menston 41,91; Northowram 51,91; Otley 41,91; Oxenhope 41,91; Pool 41.

Trinity Library, Bradford College.
51-71: Bradford (detailed list at Society of Genealogists).

Ilkley Library.
51-91: Addingham, Burley, Ilkley (also 41), Menston.
91: Askwith, Barden, Beamsley, Bolton Abbey, Bradleys Both, Denton, Draughton, Farnhill, Kildwick, Middleton, Nesfield with Langbar, Otley, Silsden, Weston.

Shipley Library.
41-91: Local area.
91: Eccleshill, Heaton, Idle.

Keighley Library.
41-91: Bingley; Cottingley; Cullingworth; Harden; Haworth; Keighley; Morton; Oxenhope; Silsden; Steeton with Eactburn; Sutton.
81,91: Kildwick/Farnhill.
Street Indexes: available for all the above plus surname indexes 1841-1881 for Keighley.

Calderdale Central Library, Halifax.
41-91: Barkisland, Clifton-cum-Hartshead, Ellan-cum-Greetland, Erringden, Fixby, Halifax, Heptonstall, Hipperholme-cum-Brighouse, Langfield, Midgley, Norland, Northowram, Ovendon, Rastrick, Rishworth, Shelf, Skircoat, Southowram, Sowerby, Soyland, Stainland, Stansfield, Todmorden-cum-Walsden, Wadsworth, Warley.

Yorkshire: West Riding continued

Huddersfield Central Library (Kirklees MB)
41-91: Kirklees Metropolitan area, incl.
Huddersfield.

Huddersfield Polytechnic.
51: Allerton, N Bierley, Bolton, Bowling, Bradford, Calverley with Farsley, Clayton, Cleckheaton, Drighlington, Eccleshill, Heaton, Horton, Hunsworth, Idle, Manningham, Pudsey, Shipley, Thornton, Tong, Wilsden, Wyke.

Batley Library.
Adwalton 41; E and W Ardsley 41; Batley 41-91; Birkenshaw 41; Birstall 41,71-91; Briestfield 51; Chickenley 51,61,71; Chidswell 91; Churwell 41; Dewsbury 41; Cleckheaton 41; Crofton 41; Drighlington 41; Earlsheaton 51-81; Emley 41; Gawthorpe 41,51; Gildersome 41; Gomersal 41,71,81; Grange Moor 51; Heckmondwike 51; Hightown 51; Littletown 51; Liversedge 51; Morley (pt) 41-61; Oakenshaw 41; Ossett 41,51; Roberttown 51; Scholes 41; Shaw Cross 91; Staincliffe 61,71,91; Thornhill 51; Thornhill Lees 51; Whitley Lower 51.

Cleckheaton Library.
41-91: E and N Bierley, Birkenshaw, Birstall, Cleckheaton, Gomersal, Hartshead, Heckmondwike, Hunsworth, Liversedge, Wyke.

Dewsbury Library.
Batley Carr 61; Dewsbury 41-91; Nether Soothill 41-81; Thornhill 41-9; Lower Whitley 71,81.

SOUTH YORKSHIRE (post-1974)

Sheffield Archives, 52 Shoreham Street, Sheffield.
41-81: present county of **South Yorkshire**, incl. Barnsley, Doncaster, Rotherham and Sheffield.
91: Sheffield and the immediate vicinity, including West, North and South Sheffield, Sheffield Park, Brightside, Attercliffe, Handsworth, Nether Hallam, Upper Hallam, Norton, Ecclesall Bierlow, Cawthorne, High Hoyland, Penistone, Wortley, Ecclesfied and Bradfield.
91: West Riding: Cawthorne, High Hoyland, Penistone, Wortley, Ecclesfield, Bradfield.
Indexes: surnames 41-71Ecclesfield/Bradfield 51-71, Penistone 71, Barnsley 41-81; streets 41-91.
   See pamphlet *Census Returns: Sheffield Record Office* for full list of all places and reel numbers.

Barnsley Central Library.
41-91: Barnsley and area (missing years bracketed): Ackworth (41), Adwick upon Dearne, Ardsley, Barmbrough, Barnsley, Barugh, Billingley, Blacker (51), Bloomhouse Green (51), Bolton-upon-Dearne, Monk Bretton, Brierley, Broadroyd Head, Brodsworth, Bromley, Broomhill, Cadeby, Carlton, Carr Green (51), Cawthorne, Clayton, Club Gardens or Row (Darton), Cudworth, Cusworth, Darfield, Darton, Denby (also Dale and Lr), Dodworth, Dodworth Bottom (71), Ecklands, N and S Elmsall (41),

Barnsley Central Library continued
Elsecar, Finkel Street, Foulby (41), Frickley, Gawber, Goldthorpe, Grimethorpe, Gunthwaite, Hamhall Stubbs (41), W Hardwick (41), Havercroft (71), Hickleton (41), Cold and S Hiendley, Higham, Hodroyd, Hooton Pagnell (41), Gt and Lit Houghton, Howbrook, Hoyland, Hoylandswaine, Hoyle Mill, Hunshelf, Huntwick (41), Ingbirchworth, Jump, Keresforth Hill, Kexborough, Kingstone Place, S Kirkby (41), Kitroyd (41), Langsett, Mapplewell (51), Marr (41), High Melton (41), Nostell (41), Notton, Oxspring, Penistone, Pigburn (41), Pilley, Pogmoor, Roughbirchwood, Royston, Ryhill, Scissett (41), Shaton, Silkstone (41), Smithies, Sprotbrough, Stainborough, Staincross (51), Stairfoot (41), Swithen, Tankersley (41), Thurgoland, Thurlstone, Thurnscoe (41), Wintersett, Wombwell, Woolley, Worsbrough, Wortley.
Also some places for single years.
Additions: Clayton West 41-91; High Hoyland 41-91; Stocksbridge, Thorpe Hesley, Wath upon Dearne 41 & 91; Wentworth 41,91.
Index: Barnsley 41-81, incl. shortened transcripts of entries etc (copy also at *Sheffield Archives*).

Central Library and Arts Centre, Rotherham.
41-91: whole of **Rotherham** Metropolitan Borough, plus a few parishes just over the boundary.
Indexes: Rotherham RD 51 (formerly held at South Yorkshire R.O.); Rotherham area, 81, in progress.

Doncaster Central Library.
41-81: Doncaster Metropolitan area (detailed list with Society of Genealogists).
91: Adwick le Street; Adwick upon Dearne, Almholme; Alverley; Arksey; Armthorpe; Askern; Auckley; Austerfield; Balby (with Hexthorpe); Barnburgh; Barnsdale Bar; Barnby Dun; Bawtry; Bentley (with Arksey); Bessacarr; Bilham; Blaxton; Braithwaite; Braithwell; Bramwith Woodhouse; Branton; Brodsworth; Burghwallis; Cadeby; Campsall; Cantley; Carcroft; Carr House; Clayton with Frickley;; Conisbrough; Cusworth; Denaby; Doncaster; Dunscroft; Edenthorpe; Edlington; Fenwick; Finningley; Fishlake; Frickley; Hampole; Harlington; Hatfield; Hatfield Woodhouse; Haywood; Hexthorpe; Hickleton; High Melton; Holme; Hooton Pagnell; Kirk Bramwith; Kirk Sandall; Kirkhouse green; Langthwaite with Tilts; Levitt Hagg; Littleworth; Long Sandall (with Wheatley); Loversall; Marr; Mexborough; Moorends; Moorhouse; Moss; Newton; Norton; Owston; Pigburn (Pickburn); Rossington; Sandall Brickyards; Scawsby; Scawthorpe; Shaftholme; Skellow; Sprotbrough; Stainforth; Stainton; Stancil; Stotfold; Sutton; Sykehouse; Thorne; Thrpe in Balne; Tickhill; Tilts; Wadworth; Warmsworth; Wellingley; Wheatley; Wilsic.

Hull Central Library.
51: Selby district, with villages index.

Scunthorpe Central Library (Humberside C.C.).
51-91: Thorne Registration District.

Yorkshire: West Riding continued

Nottinghamshire Local Studies Library, Nottingham.
Anston 51,81; Dinnington 51; Firbeck 51,81;
Gildingwells 81; Hardwick 51; Harthill 51,81; Kiveton
Park 81; Laughton-en-le-Morthen 51; Letwell 81;
Thorpe Salvin 51,81; Throapham 81; Todwick
51,81; Wales 51,81; Wales Bar 81; Waleswood 81;
Woodsetts 51,81.

Nottinghamshire Record Office, Nottingham.
51: same places as Notts. Co. Lib.

Lancashire Libraries, libraries at Barnoldswick (B),
Nelson (N).
4 = 1841, 5 = 1851; 6 = 1861; 7 = 1871; 8 =1881, 9
= 1891.
Addingham N48; Appletreewick N48; Arncliffe N48;
Bank Newton B45,N458; Barden N48; Bolton Abbey
N48; Bradley's Booth N58; Buckden B45,N458;
Burnsall N48; Carlton (nr Skipton) N48; Cold
Coniston B45,N458; Coniston with Kilnsey
B45,N458; Cracoe N48; Eslack N48; Embsay with
Eastby N48; Eshton B45,N458; Farnhill N58;
Flashby B45,N458; Gargrave B45,N458;
Grassington N48; Hawkswick N48; Hebden N48;
Hetton-with-Doardley B45,N458; Kettlewell N58;
Kildwick N58; Linton and Linton Mill N48; Rilston
N48; Starbottom N58; Thorpe N48; Threshfield N48.

Lancaster Library.
41: Ainton, Halton West, Hanlith, Hellifield, Kirkby
Malham, Malham, Otterburn, Scasthrop.

Lancashire Record Office, Preston.
51,61: Bashall Eaves, Bolton-by-Bowland, Lr and Hr
Bowland Forest, Lit Bowland, W Bradford,
Easington, Gisburn, Gisburn Forest, Grindleton,
Horton, Middop, Newton, Paythorn, Rimington,
Sawley, Slaidburn, Waddington.
41: pre 1974 county of Lancashire.
See also *Clitheroe Library*, under Lancashire.

Oldham Library.
41-91: Saddleworth.

Derby Central Library, Local Studies Dept.,
Abbeydale 81; Aughton 51,91; Auston 51;
Backmoor 18,91; Beauchief 51,71,81,91; Beighton
41,51,71,91; Birks 51; Birley 51; Bradway 51,81,91;
Brampton 51; Brampton-le-Morthen 91; Brinsworth
51; Broom 51; Canklow 51; Catcliffe 51,71,81,91;
Dinnington 51; Dore 41,51,71,81; Fence 51,91;
Firbeck 51; Gildingwells 51; Hackenthorpe 51,91;
Harthill 51; Hemsworth 81,91; Herringthorpe 51;
Kiveton 51; Letwell 51; Moorgate 51; Moorhouse 51;
Mosborough 41-91; North Auston 51; Norton 51,81;
Norton nr Sheffield 41,51,71; Norton Hammer
51,81; Norton Lees 51,81,91; Roaks Moor 51;
Rotherham 51; Sheffield 51; South Anston 51;
Swallows Nest 51,91; Thorpe Salvin 51; Tinsley 51;
Todwick 51; Toltley 41,51,71,81; Treeton 71-91;
Ulley 51,71,81,91; Unthank 41,51,71,81; Upper
Hallam, Wales 51; Wickersley 51; Woodall 51;
Woodseats 51,81; Woodsetts 51.

Derbyshire County Library, Matlock.
41-91: Parishes bordering Derbyshire including:-
Abbeydale, Aston, Aughton, Birley Moor and Vale,
Dolehill, Brampton en le Morthen, Carr Forge,
Catcliffe, Fence, Fullwood, Upper Hallam, Millstone
Hill, Rainbow Forge, Ranmoor, Ringinglow, N
Staveley, Swallownest, Treeton, Ulley, Woodseats.

Kendal Library (Cumbria C.C.).
41-91: Sedbergh area (incl Garsdale, Dent,
Cowgill).

HUMBERSIDE

Humberside Archive Service, Beverley.
91: Goole district.

Scunthorpe Central Library.
51-91: Goole Registration District.

WALES and Monmouthshire

Publications:
The Religious Census of 1851. 1. South Wales,
1976; 2, *North Wales*, 1981, ed. I.G. Jones.

National Library of Wales, Aberystwyth.
41-91: Wales and Monmouthshire complete.

ANGLESEY

Census Index:
  See *Marriage, Census and Other Indexes.*

National Library of Wales, Aberystwyth.
41-91: complete county.

Anglesey County Record Office.
41-91: complete county.
Transcripts: Llanerchymedd 51; Llanddyfnan
41,61,71,81; Penmynydd 51.

Caernarfon and Dolgellau Record Offices.
91: complete county.

The Library, Normal College, Bangor.
41-91: complete county.

BRECKNOCKSHIRE
Now mainly in Powys.

Census Indexes:
  See *Marriage, Census and Other Indexes.*

National Library of Wales, Aberystwyth.
41-91: complete county.

Brecon Area Library HQ (Powys County Library).
41-91: complete county.

Glamorgan Record Office, Cardiff.
41-91: Vaynor, Penderyn, Ystradfellte,
Ystradgynlais.
91: Crickhowell RD.

Merthyr Tydfil Central Library.
41-91: Cefn Coed, Ponsticill.

CAERNARVONSHIRE

Census Indexes and Publications:
  See *Marriage, Census and Other Indexes.*

National Library of Wales, Aberystwyth.
41-91: complete county.

Caernarfon Record Office
41-91: complete county.

Anglesey County and Dolgellau Record Offices.
91: complete county.

The Library, Normal College, Bangor.
41-91: complete county.

Denbighshire and Flintshire Record Offices.
51-91: a few parishes bordering Denbighshire
(including Llandudno 51 and 71).

CARDIGANSHIRE

Census Indexes:
  See *Marriage, Census and Other Indexes* for
Dyfed FHS 1851 census index project. Indexed
transcripts to most of **north Cardiganshire,
1841-1881,** are at the *National Library of Wales,
Ceredigion Record Office,* and *Aberystwyth Public
Library.*

National Library of Wales, Aberystwyth.
41-91: complete county.

Ceredigion Record Office, Aberystwyth.
41-91: complete county.

Aberystwyth Public Library.
91: Cardiganshire.
Indexed transcripts: Aberystwyth 41-91;
Broncastellan and Clarach 51; Cardigan 51; Ceulan
y Maesmawr, Cynnullmawr and Elerch 41-81;
Llanafan, Llanbadarn y Creuddyn and Llanfihangel
y Creuddyn 41; North Cardiganshire 41-81;
Lampeter 51; Ysgubor y Coed 41-81.

CARMARTHENSHIRE
Now part of Dyfed.

Census Indexes and Publications:
  See *Marriage, Census and Other Indexes* for
Dyfed FHS 1851 census index publications.

National Library of Wales, Aberystwyth.
41-91: complete county.

Carmarthen Public Library.
41-91: complete county.
Name indexes: 41 Llanllwni and Llanybydder; 51
Carmarthen (town) and Llanelli.

Carmarthenshire Record Office, Carmarthen.
81: Carmarthenshire (photocopy and Mormon
index).

Llanelli Public Library.
41-91: Llanelli and neighbourhood (Commote of
Carnwallon).

Pembrokeshire Record Office, Haverfordwest.
51-81: some border parishes, incl. Llanboidy,
Cilmaenllwyd, Eglwysfairachurig, Pendine and
Marros.

Glamorgan Record Office, Cardiff.
51-81: Llangennech.
51-71: Llanelli.

DENBIGHSHIRE

National Library of Wales, Aberystwyth.
41-91: complete county.

Denbighshire Record Office, Ruthin.
41-91: complete county.
Note. Missing, 41: Wrexham, Gresford, Marchwiel, Ruabon, Erbistock and Holt (Bromfield hundred) but the Record Office has a MS return for Wrexham town (DD/DM/228/62), see County Archivist's Annual report 1977; Clocaenog, Derwen, Llanarmon-yn-Ial and Nantglyn.
Incomplete, 41: Llanelidan, Llanfair Dyffryn Clwyd.
Missing, 61: Betws yn Rhos, Derwen, Efenechtyd, Llanarmon Mynydd Mawr, Llanddulas, Llanelidan, Llanfair Dyffryn Clwyd, Llanfihangel Glyn Myfyr, Llanefydd and St. George.

Flintshire Record Office, Hawarden, Deeside.
41-91: parishes bordering on Flintshire.
Note. Missing 41: Erbistock, Gresford, Holt, Isycoed, Marchweil, Ruabon.

University College of Wales (Dept. of Geography), Aberystwyth.
Wrexham 41-71 (41 photocopy of *Clwyd R.O.* copy).

Shropshire Records & Research Centre, Shrewsbury.
41-91: Places in Denbighshire near Ellesmere and Oswestry.

FLINTSHIRE

Census Indexes:
  See *Marriage, Census and Other Indexes* for 1841 and 1851 census indexes.

National Library of Wales, Aberystwyth.
41-91: complete county.

Flintshire Record Office, Hawarden, Deeside.
41-91: complete county.
Note. Missing, 41: Bangor, Hope, Llanfynydd, Marford and Hoseley, Treuddyn, Worthenbury.
Missing, 61: Cilcain, Gwaenysgor.
Incomplete, 61: Various parishes appear to be incomplete.
Missing, 71: Bangor, Iscoed.

Denbighshire Record Office, Ruthin.
51-81: a few parishes bordering Denbighshire.

Shropshire Records & Research, Shrewsbury.
41-91: Places in Flintshire near Ellesmere and Whitchurch.

Cambridgeshire Record Office, Cambridge.
81: Flintshire (Mormon index).

GLAMORGAN
Now split between West Glamorgan, Mid Glamorgan and South Glamorgan.

Census Indexes and Publications:
  See *Marriage, Census and Other Indexes* for Glamorgan FHS and other census index projects and publications, 1841-1881.

National Library of Wales, Aberystwyth.
41-91: complete county.

Glamorgan Record Office, Cardiff.
41-91: complete county.
Name indexes:
41: Cardiff, Llanfabon, Llantwit Major; 51: most of the county of Glamorgan; 61-81: Llanfabon, Llantwit Major; 61-71: Roath; 91: Penarth.

South Glamorgan County Library, Cardiff.
41: Hundreds of Cowbridge, Dinas Powis, Kibbor (which includes Cardiff), Miskin, Ogmore and Cardiff Borough (St John and St Mary).
51-81: RDs of Cardiff and Bridgend (only parts which are now in the present county of South Glamorgan).
91: Registration Districts of Cardiff and of Bridgend (mainly the parts of which are now in the present county of South Glamorgan but including some sub-districts now in the present county of Mid-Glamorgan).
Surname indexes: 41,51, Cardiff (St. John and St. Mary), Llandaff and Roath.

Welsh Folk Museum, St. Fagans, Cardiff.
41: Dinas-Powis Hundred.
51: Cardiff SD.
61,71: Lavernock, Llandough, Radyr, Penarth, St. Fagans.
61 only: Cairau, Cogan, Leckwith, Michaelstone-le-Pit.

University College, Cardiff.
51-81: Cardiff district (also index 51 as at *South Glamorgan County Library, Cardiff*). Open 9am-10pm in term and Saturday mornings, 9-5 in vacation. Microprinter available.

Mid-Glamorgan County Library HQ, Bridgend.
41-81: all RDs in Mid-Glamorgan. Policy is now to make available census returns to local areas rather than at one central point. Therefore the following libraries hold census to their own areas:
Bargoed Library, Bridgend Library, Pontypridd Library: **41-91.**
Pyle Library, Maesteg Library, Llantrisant Library, Rhymney Library, Nelson Library: **41-81.**

Cynon Valley Central Library, Aberdare.
Aberdare 41-91; Gellygaer 51; Llanfabon 51-81; Llantrisant 41; Llantwit Fardre 41; Llanwonno 41 (incl. Mountain Ash, Abercynon, Ynysybwl) 41-91; Penderyn 51,81; Pentyrch 41; Radyr 41; Ystradfodwg 41,61,81,91;
Name index: Aberdare 41,51; Llanwonno 51.

Glamorgan continued

Merthyr Tydfil Central Library.
41: Merthyr Tydfil (Dowlais missing, Upper Merthyr RD no known location).
51: Whole of Merthyr Tydfil RD including Aberdare.
61,71: Whole of Merthyr Tydfil except Aberdare.
81,91: Whole of Merthyr Tydfil including Gellideg, Bargoed, Hengoed, Fochriw, Gelligaer, Trelewis.
41-91: Llanfabon parish.

Treorchy Library, Rhondda, Mid-Glamorgan.
41-91: Llantrisant, Llanwonno, Ystradyfodwg.
41-61: Clydach, Penderyn, Pentyrch, Rhigos.
41-81: Llanfabon.
41,51: Aberdare, Llantwitvardre; SDs of Caerphilly and St. Nicholas.
41: Radyr, Cefnpennar, Cwmdare, Forchaman, Llwydcoed, Treforest.

West Glamorgan Record Office, Swansea.
41: Gower.
51: Aberdare, Bridgend, Cadoxton-juxta-Neath, Caerphilly, Cardiff, Cilybebyll, Cowbridge, Gelligaer, Gower, Llanfabon, Llangiwg, Llangyfelach, Llansamlet, Llantrisant, Llanwonno, Loughor, Maesteg, Merthyr Lower, Merthyr Tydfil, Pontypridd, St. Nicholas, St. Woolos, Swansea Town, Ystradgynlais.
81: Gower East, Gower West, Loughor, Oystermouth.
91: Margam.

Swansea Central Library (Reference Dept).
41-91: West Glamorgan.

University College of Swansea.
41: Hundreds of Swansea, Llangyfelach.
51: SDs of Llandilo-Talybont, Llangyfelach.
61: SDs of Swansea and Gower.
71: SDs of Swansea, Llangyfelach and Gower.
81: RG 11/5350-5369.
91: RG 12/4470-4490.

MERIONETH

Census Indexes and Publications
See *Marriage, Census and Other Indexes* for Gwynedd FHS 1851 census index publications.

National Library of Wales, Aberystwyth.
41-91: complete county.

Dolgellau Record Office.
41-91: complete county.

Anglesey County and Caernarfon Record Offices
91: complete county.

Denbighshire and Flintshire Record Offices, Hawarden and Ruthin.
41-91: Betws Gwerfil Goch, Corwen, Gwyddelwern, Llandrillo-yn-Edeyrnion, Llangar and Llansanffraid Glyndyfrwy (Edeyrnion hundred).

MONMOUTHSHIRE
Now Gwent in Wales.

National Library of Wales, Aberystwyth.
41-91: complete county.

Newport Reference Library (Newport Libraries).
41-91: complete county.

Gwent Record Office, Cwmbran.
91: complete county.

Gloucestershire Record Office.
51: Caerwent, Caldicote, Chapel Hill, Chepstow, Dingestow, Itton, Kilgurrug, Llanfairdiscoed, Llanfihangel Roggiett, Llanfihangel Torynnynyod, Llanfihangel Ystern Llewern, Llangattock, Llangurnuchan, Llansoy, Llantillio Crosseny, Mathern, Mounton, Netherwent, E and W Newchurch, Penrose, Penterry, Portskewett, Rockfield, Roggiett, St Arvans, St Maughans, St Pierre, Shirenewton, Skenfreth, Tintern, Tregare, Trelleck, Undy, Vibon Abel, Wolves Newton.

MONTGOMERYSHIRE
Now part of Powys.

National Library of Wales, Aberystwyth.
41-91: complete county.

Newtown Area Library (Powys County Library).
41-91: complete county.

Denbighshire and Flintshire Record Offices, Ruthin and Hawarden.
61,81-91: a few parishes bordering Denbighshire.

Shropshire Records & Research, Shrewsbury.
41-91: Chirbury SD.

PEMBROKESHIRE

Census Indexes and Publications:
See *Marriage, Census and Other Indexes.*

National Library of Wales, Aberystwyth.
41-91: complete county.

Pembrokeshire Record Office, Haverfordwest.
41-91: complete county.

RADNORSHIRE
Now part of Powys.

National Library of Wales, Aberystwyth.
41-91: complete county.

Powys Library Service HQ, Llandrindod Wells.
41-91: complete county.

Hereford Library.
61: Presteigne and Knighton districts.
71: New and Old Radnor, Glascum, Gladestry, Llandegley, Evenjobb, Walton, Michaelchurch on Arrow.

Hereford and Worcester R.O., Hereford Branch.
91: Radnorshire.

Shropshire Records & Research, Shrewsbury.
41-91: Knighton district.

ISLE OF MAN

Manx Museum Library, Manx National Heritage, Douglas.
41-91: Isle of Man complete.

Aberdeen Family History Shop (Aberdeen & N.E. Scotland FHS), 164 King St, Aberdeen AB2 3BD.
81: Isle of Man.

Publications:
See *The Manx Family Tree: A Beginners Guide to Records in The Isle of Man,* by Janet Narasimham, 1994.
Name Indexes:
1891, IoM FHS (1992).
1851, 1881. Transcripts (IoM FHS).

CHANNEL ISLANDS
JERSEY

The Jersey Library, Halkett Place, St. Helier.
41-91: Jersey.
Indexes: St. Helier 51,71; all parishes except St. Helier 61.

Société Jersiaise, 7 Pier Road, St. Helier.
41-91: Jersey.
Indexes: Jersey 41-91;

Aberdeen Family History Shop (as above).
81: Jersey.

GUERNSEY

The Greffe, Royal Court House, Guernsey.
41-91: Guernsey, Alderney, Sark.

Priaulx Library, Candie Rd, St Peter Port, Guernsey.
41-91: Guernsey.
Indexes: 91 in process of indexing.

Société Jersiaise, 7 Pier Road, St. Helier.
91: Guernsey.

Aberdeen Family History Shop (as above).
81: Guernsey.

SCOTLAND

The original census returns for Scotland for 1841, 1851, 1861, 1871, 1881 and 1891 are available for consultation on microfilm at the *General Register Office for Scotland, New Register House, Edinburgh EH1 3YT* (tel. 031-334-0380). Work is progressing on indexes to the 1881 and 1891 censuses.

There is a search charge. The G.R.O. is in fact in West Register Street, leading off Princes Street beside the Scottish Record Office, opposite the Balmoral Hotel.

Microfilm copies of parts of the Scottish census returns are available at other locations in Scotland, as listed below.

Publications:

See *Genealogical microform holdings in Scottish Libraries*, produced by Margaret Nikolic of Kirkaldy District Libraries in 1992. A second edition is due to be published later in 1994. It is a comprehensive listing of local library microfilm holdings of the Scottish census records and the OPRS.

This supersedes *West of Scotland Census Returns and Old Parochial Registers*, 3rd edn., 1986, compiled by Anne Escott, Glasgow District Libraries, which provides parish by parish holdings in a number of West of Scotland libraries in greater detail than is possible in this Guide. It also provides county/parish maps and census enumeration district maps of Glasgow. It is available from any library in this area or from the Mitchell Library, Glasgow.

Note. As with England and Wales, this section is arranged by Scottish counties or administrative areas as they existed in the nineteenth century and up to 1974.

ABERDEENSHIRE

Aberdeen Central Library.
41-91: Aberdeenshire.

North East of Scotland Library Service, The Meadows Industrial Estate, Meldrum Meg Way, Oldmeldrum, Aberdeenshire.
41-91: Aberdeenshire excl. city district of Aberdeen.

Aberdeen Family History Shop (Aberdeen & N.E. Scotland FHS) 164 King St., Aberdeen AB2 3BD.
41-91: Aberdeenshire, all parishes and districts.
41-91: Aberdeen City.

Elgin Library (Moray District Libraries), Elgin.
Aberdour 51-71, Aboyne 41-71, Alford 41-71, Auchterless 41-71, Auchindoir 41-71, Belhelvie 41-71,91, Birse 41-71,91, Bourtie 41-71,91, Cairnie 41-81, Cabrach 91; Chapel of Garioch 41-81, Clatt 41-81, Cluny 41-81, Coull 41-81, Crathie and Braemar 51-81, Crimond 61, Cruden 61, Culsamond 61, St. Nicholas 81.

ANGUS or FORFARSHIRE

Dundee Central Library.
41-81: Dundee; Liff and Benvie; Mains and Strathmartine; Monifieth and Murroes; and a majority of Angus parishes.
91: Dundee.

Forfar Library.
41-91: Angus.

Aberdeen Family History Shop (as Aberdeens.).
41: Carmyllie,
41-51: Careston, Cortachy and Clova, Coupar Angus, Craig, Dun; Dundee (51 only); Montrose, Murroes, Newtyle, Oathlaw, Panbridge, Rescobie.

ARGYLL

Inverness Regional Library Service.
41-91: Argyll.

Dumbarton Public Library.
61,71: Acharacle, Ardchattan, Ardnamurchan, Arisaig, Ballachulish, Corran of Ardgour, Campbeltown, Craignish (61 only), Cumlodden (61 only), Dunoon and Kilmun (pt 61 only), Sunart or Strontian.

Paisley Museum.
Tiree and Coll 61,71.

AYR

Paisley Museum.
Ardrossan 41,61,71; Auchinleck 61,71; Ayr 41,51,61; Girvan 51; Saltcoats 41.

Dick Institute, Kilmarnock.
41-91: all places in **Ayrshire**.

Edinburgh Central Library.
41-91: Ayrshire.

The Mitchell Library, Glasgow.
51,91: Ardrossan, Auchinleck, Ayr, Ballantrae, Barr, Beith, Colmonell, Coylton, Craigie, Dailly, Dalmellington, Dalry, Dalrymple, Dreghorn, Dundonald, Dunlop, Fenwick, Galston, Girvan, Irvine, Kilbirnie, Kilmarnock, Kilmaurs, Kilwinning, Kirkmichael, Kirkoswald, Largs, Loudoun, Mauchline, Maybole, Monkton and Prestwick, Muirkirk, New Cumnock, Ochiltree, Old Cumnock, Riccarton, St. Quivox and Newton-on-Ayr, Sorn, Stair, Stevenston, Stewarton, Straiton, Symington, Tarbolton, West Kilbride.
91: Lungar, Barrhill, Crosshill, Troon, Cunninghame Combination Poorhouse, Patna, Hirlford.

BANFFSHIRE

Census Indexes and Publications:
An 1851 census index for Banffshire is being compiled by the Aberdeen and NE Scotland FHS and can be purchased from the Aberdeen Family History Shop, 164 King Street, Aberdeen AB2 3BD.

Elgin Library (Moray District Libraries), Elgin.
See leaflet *Tracing your Roots in Moray* which lists all parishes and census years covered.
41-91: Banffshire: Aberlour, Alvah, Banff, Botriphnie, Boyndie, Cullen, Deskford, Enzie, Fordyce, Forglen, Gamrie, Macduff, Glennrinnes, Grange, Inveravon, Glenlivet, Inverkeithny, Keith, Kirkmichael, Marnoch, Mortlach, Ordiquhill, Rathven, Rothiemay, St. Fergus and Seafield.

NE of Scotland Library Service (as Aberdeens.).
41-91: Banffshire (the major part, i.e. excluding what is now Moray district.)

Fraserburgh Library.
41-91: Banff and Buchan districts.

Aberdeen Central Library.
Marnoch 61; Mortlach 61,71; Ordiquhill 61,71; Rothiemay 41-71; Rathven 41-81.

Aberdeen Family History Shop (as Aberdeens.).
41-91: Banffshire, all parishes and districts.

BERWICKSHIRE

Borders Regional Library HQ, St Mary's Mill, Selkirk.
41-91: Berwickshire.

Edinburgh Central Library.
41-91: Berwickshire.

BUTE and ARRAN

Aberdeen Family History Shop (as Aberdeens.).
51: county of Bute.

Paisley Museum.
Arran (Brodick) 71; North Bute 61,71; Cumbraes 61,71; Kilbride 61,71; Kingarth 61; Rothesay 41,61,71.

CAITHNESS

Aberdeen Family History Shop (as Aberdeens.)
41: Caithness county, all parishes and districts.

Inverness Regional Library Service.
41-91: Caithness.

Orkney Library, Kirkwall.
Bower 41,61-81; Canisbay 41,61-81; Dunnet 41,61-81; Halkirk pt 41,61,71,pt81; Latheron pt 61,pt71; Reay and Thurso 51.

CLACKMANNANSHIRE

Clackmannan District Library, Alloa.
41-91: Clackmannanshire.

Edinburgh Central Library.
41-91: Clackmannanshire.

Falkirk Public Library.
Baldernock 41-81; Dollar 51.

DUMFRIESSHIRE

Dumfries Archive Centre, 33 Burns Street, Dumfries.
41-91: Dumfriesshire. Prior booking necessary.

Edinburgh Central Library.
41-91: Dumfriesshire.

DUNBARTONSHIRE

Dumbarton Public Library.
41-91: Dunbartonshire East and **West:** Arrochar, Bonhill, Cardross, Cumbernauld, Dumbarton, Kilmarnock, Kirkintilloch, Luss, New and Old Kilpatrick, Rosneath, Rhu.

Strathkelvin Reference Library, The William Patrick Library, 2 West High Sreet, Kirkintilloch.
Bonhill 51; Cumbernauld 51; Dumbarton 41,81; Kilmarnock 41-81; Kirkintilloch 41-81; Luss 41,61; New Kilpatrick 41-61; Old Kilpatrick 61; Rosneath 61; Row or Rhu 61.
91: Kilmarnock, Kirkintilloch.

Mitchell Library, Glasgow.
51,91: Arrochar, Bonhill, Cardross, Cumbernauld, Dumbarton, Kilmaronock, Kirkintilloch,
91: Renton, Old Kilpatrick, Roseneath, Kilcreggan and Cove, Row (Rhu).

Cumbernauld Central Library.
51-91: Cumbernauld.

EAST LOTHIAN (Haddingtonshire)

East Lothian District Library Local History Centre, Newton Port, Haddington.
41-91: East Lothian.

Edinburgh Central Library.
41-91: East Lothian.

Edinburgh see **Midlothian**
Elgin see **Moray**

FIFE

Cupar District Library.
41-91: North-east Fife.

Edinburgh Central Library.
41-91: Fife.

Kirkcaldy District Library.
41-91: Abbotshall; Aberdour; Anstruther-Easter; Anstruther-Wester; Arngask; Auchterderran; Auchtertool; Ballingry; Beath; Burntisland; Cameron; Carnbee; Carnock; Crail; Dalgety; Dumfermline; Dunino; Dysart; Elie; Falkland; Ferryport-on-Craig; Flisk; Forgan; Iverkeithing; Kemback; Kennoway; Kettle; Kilconqhar; Kilmany; Kilrenny; Kingsbarns; Largo; Leuchars; Logie; Markinch; Monimail; Moonzie; Newburgh; Newburn; Pittenweem; St. Andrews and St. Leonards; St. Monans and Abercrombie; Saline; Scoonie (not 61); Strathmiglo; Torryburn; Wemys.
51-91: Abdie; Auchtermuchty; Balmerino; Ceres; Collessie; Creich; Cults; Cupar; Dairsie; Kinghorn, Kinglassie; Kircaldy; Leslie.
61-91: Dunbog;

Forfarshire see **Angus**

GLASGOW (Lanarkshire)

Glasgow District Libraries, Mitchell Library.
41-81: Glasgow (city); Barony; Govan.
91: Glasgow (city and Barony), Cathcart, Eaglesham, Neilston, Barrhead and Levern, Cambuslang, Carluke, Carmichael, Carmunnock, Glassford, Govan, Old Monkland, Pettinain and Rutherglen.
91 (those marked with an asterisk are for 51 also): Avondale; Biggar*; Blantyre*; Bothwell*; Holytown*; Cadder (Western); Cadder (Eastern); Calderhead; Cambusnethan; Carnwath; Forth; Carstairs; Covington and Thankerton; Crawford; Leadhills; Crawfordjohn; Culter; Larkhall; Dalserf; Dalziel; Dolphington*; Douglas*; Dunsyre*; East Kilbride*; Hamilton*; Lanark*; Lesmahagow*; Libberton*; Airdrie; New Monkland*; Shotts; Stonehouse; Symington; Walston; Wandell and Lamington; Wiston and Roberton;

Strathkelvin Reference Library, Kirkintilloch.
Glasgow (Gorbals, small part) 51.
91: Cadder.

East Kilbride Central Library, The Olympia.
Barony pt 41,pt 51,pt 61; Glasgow pt 61, pt 71;
Govan 41,pt 51,pt 61, pt 71.

Hamilton District Library.
Glasgow (city; small part only) 41,71; Govan 41,61-81; pt 61,pt 71; Barony 61-81(pt).

Haddingtonshire see **East Lothian**

INVERNESS-SHIRE

Aberdeen Family History Shop (see Aberdeens.)
41: all parishes and districts.
51: Inverness district.

Inverness Public Library.
41-91: County of Inverness.

Elgin Library (Moray District Libraries), Elgin.
41-81: Abernethy and Kincardine (61 only); Kilmonivaig; Limorack; Kiltarlity; Kingussie; Kirkhill; Laggan; Moy and Dalarossie; Petty; Urquhart and Glenmoriston (41, 61 only)

Dumbarton District Library.
41-91: Arisaig, Ballachulish.

KINCARDINESHIRE

NE of Scotland Library Service (see Aberdeens.).
41-91: Kincardineshire.

Aberdeen Central Library.
41-91: Kincardineshire.

Aberdeen Family History Shop (see Aberdeens.).
41-91: Kincardineshire.

KINROSS-SHIRE

A.K. Bell Library, York Place, Perth.
41-91: Kinross-shire.

Edinburgh Central Library.
41-91: Kinross-shire.

KIRKCUDBRIGHTSHIRE

Dumfries Archive Centre, 33 Burns Street, Dumfries.
41-91: Kirkcudbrightshire. Prior booking needed.

LANARKSHIRE

Airdrie Library (Monklands District Libraries) (A);
Dumbarton Public Library (D); *Glasgow District
Libraries, Mitchell Library* (G); *Hamilton District
Library* (H); *East Kilbride Central Library* (K);
*Lindsay Institute, Lanark (Clydesdale District
Council)* (L); *Strathkelvin District Library,
Kirkintilloch* (S).
4 = 41; 5 = 51; 6 = 61; 7 = 71; 8 = 81; 9 = 91.

Avondale K4-8, Gpt4,5,pt6,pt8,9; H5; Barony: see
Glasgow, above; Biggar G5-9; H6-9; K4-7, L5-8;
Blantyre H4-9,K4-8, Gpt56-9; Bothwell H4-9, K4-7,
Gpt5,6,pt7,Pt9; Cadder S4-7,pt8,9, K4-7, H4,pt6,7;
G5,pt6,89; Cambuslang K4-8, G458, H4,pt7;
Cambusnethan K456, G4589, S46, Hpt4,5,pt7;
Carluke K4568, G458, S46, L5-8, DHpt6,pt7;
Carmichael K4-8, G458, S4, L5-8, H67;
Carmunnock K4-8, G458, S4, H67; Carnwath K4-7,
L5-8, G59,H67; Carstairs K4-7, L5-8, G59, H67;
Covington and Thankerton K4-7, L5-8, G59, H67;
Crawford K4-7, L5-8, G59, H67; Crawfordjohn K4-7,
L5-8, G59, H67; Culter K4-7, H467, L5-8, G59;
Dalserf H4-9, K45,pt7, Gpt7,9; Dalziel H4-7,pt8,
K457,pt8, G579; Dolphinton K4578, H467, L5-8,
G79; Douglas K45,pt6,78, H4,pt5,pt6,7, L5-8, G79;
Dunsyre K4-8, H47, L5-8, G679; East Kilbride K4-8,
H457, G679; Glasgow: see under Glasgow, above;
Glassford K4-8, H45, G678; Govan: see Glasgow,
above; Hamilton H4-9, K45, G4,pt5,6,pt7,pt8;
Lamington see Wandell; Lanark H4,pt6,pt7,8,
A4,pt6, L5-8, Gpt69; Leadhills L5-8; Lesmahagow
H458, A46, L5-8, G59; Libberton and Quothquan
A46, H48, L5-8, G59; New Monkland A4-8, Hpt4,
G59; Old Monkland A4-8, G5,pt6,pt7; Pettinain
G4-8, A468, L5-8; Quothquan see Libberton;
Roberton L5-8; Rutherglen G4-8, A468, Hpt7;
Shotts A468, G457,pt89, Hpt4,pt6,pt7,pt8;
Stonehouse H4-9, G4579, K5, A6,pt8; Symington
G4-79, H46-9, L5-8, A6; Thankerton see Covington;
Walston G4579, H46-9, L5-8, A6; Wandell and
Lamington H46-9, G4579, L5-8, A6; Wiston and
Roberton G4579, H46-9, L5-8, A6.

Aberdeen Family History Shop (see Aberdeens.).
51: Old Monkland.

Linlithgow see **West Lothian**

MIDLOTHIAN (Edinburgh)

*Edinburgh Central Library (Scottish Department),
George IV Bridge, Edinburgh.*
41-91: Midlothian.

Borders Regional Library HQ. St.Mary's Mill, Selkirk.
91: Parishes of Fala and Soutra, Glencorse, Heriot,
Stow, Temple and West Calder.

*East Lothian District Library Local History Centre,
Newton Port, Haddington.*
41-91: parish of Inveresk.

MORAY or ELGIN

*Local Studies Section, Elgin Library (Moray District
Libraries), High Street, Elgin.*
See leaflet *Tracing your Roots in Moray.*
41-91: Moray complete.

NE of Scotland Library Service (see Aberdeens.).
41-91: some coverage of border parishes on the
Moray district boundary.

NAIRN

Aberdeen Family History Shop (see Aberdeens.).
41-81: Nairnshire.

Inverness Public Library.
41-91: Nairnshire.

Elgin Library (Moray District Libraries).
41-91: Nairnshire.

ORKNEY

Aberdeen Family History Shop (see Aberdeens.).
41: Orkney.
51: Orphir, Walls and Flotta, South Ronaldsway and
Burray.

Orkney Archives, Laing Street, Kirkwall.
41-91: Orkney.
Shetland: Foula 71,81; Papa Stour 71,81;
Sandness 71,81; Sandsting and Aithsting 51,71;
Tingwall 51,71; Unst 51,71; Walls 51,71; Whiteness
and Weisdale 51,71; North Yell and Fetlar 51.

PEEBLES

Borders Regional Library HQ, St Mary's Mill, Selkirk.
41-91: Peebleshire.

Edinburgh Central Library.
41-91: Peebleshire.

PERTHSHIRE

A.K. Bell Library, York Place, Perth.
41-91: Perthshire, incl. former Western District,
now in Stirling District.

Clackmannan District Library, Alloa.
41-91: Muckhart parish, Tulliallon parish, Logie
parish (split between Perthshire, Stirlingshire and
Clackmannanshire).
91: Glendevon parish.

Hamilton District Library.
Longforgan 81.

RENFREWSHIRE

Paisley Museum.
41-91: Renfrewshire complete.

Mitchell Library, Glasgow.
Abbey pt 51,pt 71; Barrhead and Levern 81; Busby 91; Cathcart 41-81; Eaglesham 41-81; Eastwood 41-81; Erskine 51,71,81; Gourock 91; Greenock (pt) 51,81, Houston and Killellan 51,91; Inchinnan 91; Inverkip 91; Johnstone pt81; Kilbarchan 91; Kilmacolm 91; Linwood 91; Lochwinnoch 41,51,91; Mearns 41,51; Neilston 41,51,81; Newton Mearns 91; Paisley 51,81(pt); Port Glasgow 51; Renfrew 51.

ROSS and CROMARTY

Census Indexes and Publications:
Killearnan 1851; Kiltearn 1851; Kincardine (with Croik) 1851; Knockbain 1851; £1.20 each, Tain £1.50; Wick (landward) £1.80 (+ 25p p&p) from the Highland FHS, c/o Reference Library, Farraline Park Library, Inverness.

Inverness Public Library.
41-91: Ross and Cromarty.

ROXBURGHSHIRE

Borders Regional Library HQ, St Mary's Mill, Selkirk.
41-91: Roxburghshire.

SELKIRKSHIRE

Borders Regional Library HQ, St Mary's Mill, Selkirk.
41-91: Selkirkshire.

Edinburgh Central Library.
41-91: Selkirkshire.

SHETLAND

Aberdeen Family History Shop (see Aberdeens.).
41: Shetland Isles.

Shetland Archives, 44 King Harald Street, Lerwick.
41-91: Shetland.

Orkney Archives, Laing Street, Kirkwall.
Shetland: Foula 71,81; Papa Stour 71,81; Sandness 71,81; Sandsting and Aithsting pt 41,51,71; Tingwall 41,51,71; Unst 41,51,71; Walls 41,51,71; Whiteness and Weisdale pt 41,51,71; North Yell and Fetlar 51.

Tangwick Haa Museum, Shetland.
41-81: Shetland.

STIRLINGSHIRE

Stirling Central Library.
41-91: Stirlingshire.

Edinburgh Central Library.
41-91: Stirlingshire.

Falkirk Public Library.
41-81 unless shown otherwise (probably **91** also): Airth, Alva, Baldernock, Balfron, Bothkennar, Buchanan, Campsie, Carriden, Denny, Drymen, Dunipace, Falkirk, Fintry (not 51), Gargunnock (not 51,81), Killearn (not 51,81), Kilsyth (not 51,81), Kippen (not 51,81), Larbert, Muiravonside, Polmont, St Ninians (not 51,81), Slammanan, Stirling (not 61,81), Strathblane (not 61,81),

Dumbarton Public Library.
Airth 41-81; Alva 41-81; Baldernock 41-91; Balfron 41-91; Bothkennar 41-91; Buchanan 41-91; Campsie 41-91; Denny 41-91; Drymen 41-91; Dunipace 41-19; Falkirk 41,61,71,81; Fintry 41-91; Gargunnock 41-91; Grangemouth 81,91; Haggs (Denny) 81,91; Killearn 41-91; Kilsyth 41-91; Kippen 41-91; Larbert 41,71; Muiravonside 41,71; Polmont 41,71; Slammanan 41,51,pt71,71; St. Ninian's 41,71; Stirling 41-91; Strathblane 41-91.

Strathkelvin District Libraries, Kirkintilloch.
Airth 61-81; Alva 61-81; Baldernock 41-91; Balfron 41-91; Bothkennar 41,61-91; Buchanan 41-91; Campsie 41-91; Denny 41,61-81; Drymen 41-71; Dunipace 41,61,71; Fintry 51; Gargunnock 51; Killearn 51; Kilsyth 51; Kippen 51; Muiravonside 51; New Kilpatrick 51; Strathblane 51.

Clackmannan District Library, Alloa.
41-91: Alva.

Cumbernauld Central Library.
51-91: Kilsyth.

SUTHERLAND

Inverness Public Library.
41-91: Sutherland.

Aberdeen Family History Shop (see Aberdeens.).
41: Sutherland.
61: Inverness, Kilmonivaig, Kilmorack, Kiltarlity, Kingussie, Insett, Kirkhill.

WEST LOTHIAN (Linlithgow)

Edinburgh Central Library.
41-91: West Lothian.

Falkirk Public Library.
Abercorn 41-71; Bathgate 41-71; Borrowstouness (Bo'ness) 41-81; Dalmeny 41-81; Ecclesmachen 41-81; Kirkliston 41-81; Linlithgow 41-61; Livingston 41; Queensferry 41; Torpichen 41; Uphall 41; Whitburn 41.

Hamilton District Library.
Abercorn 41-71; Bathgate 41,61; Borrowstouness (Bo'ness) 41 pt 61; Carriden 41; Dalmeny 41; Ecclesmachen 41;

Mitchell Library, Glasgow.
51: Queensferry, Torpichen, Uphall, Whitburn.

WIGTOWNSHIRE

Dumfries Archive Centre, 33 Burns Street, Dumfries.
41-91: Wigtownshire. Prior booking necessary.

IRELAND

Most census returns were lost when the Irish Record Office, Dublin was destroyed in 1922.

National Archives, Bishop Street, Dublin.
1841: Co.Cavan, one parish; Co. Fermanagh, two parishes.
1851: Co. Antrim, 14 Parishes.
The returns are incomplete for some of the parishes mentioned above. Also held, paper and microfilm copies of some miscellaneous 1813-1851 Census returns.
1901: Original returns.
1911: Held but have not so far been microfilmed.

County DERRY

Research Centre, Derry Youth and Community Workshop, 10 Bishop Street, Derry, Northern Ireland BT48 6PW.
1901: Derry City and part of Co. Derry.

Mr Terry Burns informs us as follows:

"The Mormon Family History Centres can obtain for patrons of their Centres microfilm of the **1901** Census of **Ireland** as indeed they can for all filmed Censuses (1891 and earlier), Scottish, English and Welsh. The film has to be hired usually at around £2 a reel (as of September 1992). The indexes to the films are kept at the Centres. The Irish Census is on 1,173 reels so doing the whole of Ireland could be an expensive business!

"See *Fiche Family History Library* 26 Feb 1992 0001-0527 where the film numbers dealing with each County are specified. Other fiches allow an area to be more closely identified with a particular film.

"Counties covered are:
Antrim, Armagh, Carlow, Cavan, Clare, Cork, Londonderry, Donegal, Down, Dublin, Fermanagh, Galway, Kerry, Kildare, Kilkenny, King's (Offaly), Leitrim, Limerick, Longford, Louth, Mayo, Meath, Monaghan, Queen's (Leix), Roscommon, Sligo, Tipperary, Tyrone, Waterford, Westmeath, Wicklow, Wexford."